Richard Harvey Phelps

Newgate of Connecticut

Its origin and early history: Being a full description of the famous and wonderful Simsbury mines and caverns, and the prison built over them: To which is added a relation of all the incidents, insurrections, and massacres

Richard Harvey Phelps

Newgate of Connecticut

Its origin and early history: Being a full description of the famous and wonderful Simsbury mines and caverns, and the prison built over them: To which is added a relation of all the incidents, insurrections, and massacres

ISBN/EAN: 9783744751131

Printed in Europe, USA, Canada, Australia, Japan

Cover: Foto ©ninafisch / pixelio.de

More available books at **www.hansebooks.com**

NEWGATE OF CONNECTICUT;

ITS

ORIGIN AND EARLY HISTORY.

BEING A FULL DESCRIPTION OF THE
FAMOUS AND WONDERFUL SIMSBURY MINES AND CAVERNS,
AND THE PRISON BUILT OVER THEM.

TO WHICH IS ADDED

A RELATION OF ALL THE INCIDENTS, INSURRECTIONS, AND MASSACRES, CONNECTED WITH THEIR USE AS A PRISON FOR THE TORIES DURING THE REVOLUTION, AND OTHERWISE; WITH INTERESTING SKETCHES OF THEIR SURROUNDINGS,
IN (NOW) EAST GRANBY.

ALSO,

AN ILLUSTRATED DESCRIPTION OF THE
STATE PRISON AT WETHERSFIELD.

BY
RICHARD H. PHELPS.

PREFACE.

During the Autumn of 1926, the undersigned purchased the historic Newgate Prison property located at East Granby, Connecticut, at Public Auction from the Estate of Almon B. Phelps who had long been its owner. I also have discovered and purchased the electrotype plates used in printing the History of Newgate of Connecticut, by Richard H. Phelps. The last edition of this quaint and estimable work has become exhausted and I have, therefore, caused another edition to be printed and presented to the reader herewith.

The fire-swept and time-ravaged ruins of Old Newgate form doubtless one of the most interesting relics of antiquity of which New England can boast. Surely, in Connecticut, no stone ruin can be found to compare with Newgate.

Teeming, as this spot does, with tragic incident and historic lore, it cannot fail to impress the visitor, and ever remain an object of interest to the intelligent traveler. Underneath this site, the first chartered English Mining Company in America dug for copper. On this spot, the first Connecticut Colonial Prison was established. Here also, are the ruins of the first State's Prison in the State of Connecticut, and, in the abandoned Prison buildings, for a time after 1826, was manufactured the first safety fuse made anywhere in America.

Surely, the story of this historic spot and the tales of its riots, insurrections and massacres, is worthy of further preservation and dissemination.

CLARENCE W. SEYMOUR.
Hartford, Connecticut, April 1, 1927.

NEWGATE OF CONNECTICUT.

Origin of its Title—Our Puritan Ancestors—The Mines of Simsbury—Granby and Copper Hill... 13

MINING.

Discovery of Copper—The First Company Organized—Three Clergymen Appointed Smelters—Their Unsuccessful Efforts—The Proprietors are disgusted—An Act passed to regulate the Mines—King George's right to a Royalty Acknowledged—The Work Abandoned. 14

GRANBY COPPERS.

Coins made from Granby Metal—Mr. Higleys's Operations—The Sledgehammer and the Crown—Colonial Bills of Credit—Provision Pay—Prompt Payment of the Colonial Bills............................ 19

RECENT MINING.

The Old Mines Re-opened—The Phœnix Mining Co.—The Connecticut Copper Company—Depreciated Continental Currency—Curious letter a Century Old—Analysis of the Copper Ore—Silliman's Survey of the Mines.. 23

IMPRISONMENT OF THE TORIES.

The Mine transformed into a Dungeon—Prison Discipline—Whipping the Prisoners—The Tories Incarcerated—Troubles of the Revolutionary War—The Committee of Safety—The Reward of Loyalty—Opinions of a Century Ago...................................... 25

THE FIRST KEEPER OF NEWGATE.

Captain John Viets—His Little Bill for a Year—Conspiracy of the Prisoners—Locking in the Janitor—Flight and Pursuit—Strengthening the Jail.. 32

CONTENTS.

ANOTHER ESCAPE.

Burning the Block-house—Suffocated in Prison—Carelessness of the Officers.. 35

A SCENE OF CONFLICT AND BLOOD.

The Multitude of Guards Appointed—The Tories become Desperate—They Conspire to Escape—They overpower the Guard, and all Escape—Recapture of the Fugitives—The *Gazetteer* of 1773—A Cotemporary Story—The Prison buildings Destroyed............ 36

A TORY CLERGYMAN IN NEWGATE.

He Preaches a Fiery Sermon—Addresses Gen. Washington—Denounces the Whigs—Suggests the Assassination of Washington and the M. C's... 41

THE GOSPEL FURNISHED BY THE STATE.

Primitive Services—Nail-shop Preaching—Brother Jonathan Appealed To—Gen. Washington sends some "Atrocious Villains" to the Mines—Tory Misdemeanors...................................... 52

OLD NEWGATE PRISON.

The "Stone Jug"—Buildings Above-Ground—Appearance of the Caverns—Story of a Visitor—Daily Routine—More Escapes and Insurrections—Interesting Anecdotes.............................. 58

CONNECTICUT STATE PRISON.

The Building at Wethersfield—Management and Discipline—Condition of the Convicts—Notorious Instances—Facts and Statistics....... 88

HISTORICAL SKETCHES OF EAST GRANBY.

Settlements on Farmington River—Lands purchased from the Indians Trouble experienced by the Settlers—Captivity of Daniel Hayes—His Story—The Red-Men—Revolutionary Incidents—The War of 1812—The Way to reach Copper Hill................................. 116

NEWGATE OF CONNECTICUT.

———:o:———

THIS is the name by which the prison was known in the time of the American Revolution, and it was so called after Newgate prison in England. It is well known that our forefathers, in giving names to their towns and rivers, and other objects of nature and art, by which they were surrounded, drew freely upon those to which they had been accustomed in their ancestral homes; thus they endeavored to make their adopted country, in names at least, assimilate to their native land. So, in denominating this receptacle for their criminals after the world-renowned prison of London, they intended to endow it with all the terror which attached to that fearful abode of the depraved. The mines and prison buildings occupy an eminence on the western declivity of the Talcott mountain, which rises to a great elevation, and is here surmounted by lofty, precipitous and craggy rocks. This range of mountains extends through the whole length of the State, and terminates at the East Rock near New Haven. Towards the west and south, can be seen in the distance, bold and irregular outlines of mountains, interspersed with extensive valleys, forming a scene of impressive grandeur and sublimity, seldom surpassed. Says a writer:

"'The appearance of this place forcibly reminds the observer of the walls, castles, and towers, erected for the security of some haughty lordling of the feudal ages; while the gloomy dungeons within its walls, call to remembrance a Bastile, or a prison of the Inquisition."

> "A hundred legends cling about its walls,
> But silence reigns beneath its crumbling stone;
> No busy hand repairs the falling walls,
> Deserted now it wastes away alone;
> The summer idler often passes by,
> Yet some there are who enter at the gate,
> To dream awhile, and, leaving, breathe a sigh,
> To see it mouldering in such fallen state."

The mines were formerly included in the limits of the town of Simsbury, and so remained until 1786, when a part of the town, including the mines and prison, was set off and incorporated under the name of *Granby;* hence the place was at that time known by the name of *Simsbury Copper Mines,* on Copper Hill.

The town of Granby was subdivided in 1858, and the mines are at present included in the town of East Granby. If the State of Connecticut continues henceforth to increase her legislative ratio of representation by subdividing her towns, it will become difficult to trace the topography of some places within her borders, nor can it well be foreseen what town will have the honor of containing Simsbury mines at the next subdivision.

MINING.

The period at which copper ore was first discovered at this

place is not definitely known; but the first record relating to the mines, was in December 1705, when the town of Simsbury appointed a committee to make search, upon a suggestion "that there was a mine, either of silver or copper, in the town." The report of the committee is not recorded, but from subsequent results it was doubtless favorable. The first company for working the mines, was composed of land proprietors of Simsbury, in 1707. The association agreed to pay the town ten shillings on each ton of copper produced, of which two-thirds was appropriated for the support "of an able schoolmaster in Simsbury," and the other third to the "collegiate school," [Yale college]; the residue of profits was to be divided among the partners *pro rata*, according to the amount of their respective subscription shares.

All the land on Copper Hill, and in that region, was covered with the primeval forest, and occupied only as hunting ground by roving bands of Indians; and as the land was unsold, and under the control of the original proprietors of the town, the association comprised chiefly all the inhabitants. The company concluded only to dig the ore, and the first year they made a contract with three clergymen, for smelting the same, viz: John Woodbridge, of Springfield, Dudley Woodbridge, of Simsbury, and Timothy Woodbridge, Jr., of Hartford.

Clergymen at that early period were regarded as the principal embodiments of science as well as theology, and as many of them received their education in England, these contractors were supposed to possess the best facilities for obtaining information from foreign sources, in regard to the difficult process of smelting and refining. The theologians, however, did not understand the business, or at least failed to prosecute it to advantage; for in four years from their commencement, the proprietors appointed a committee to call them to account, and, if necessary, "to sue them for the ore that had been brought to them at divers times." The mines had at that time attained a good degree of celebrity, as appears by a public act passed by the colony:

> "Anno Regni Annæ Reginæ
> V. Septimo A. D. 1709."

An Act relating to the Copper Mines at Simsbury:

> "Whereas there hath lately been discovered a Copper mine at Symsbury, which hath been so improved as to give good satisfaction to conclude that a public benefit might arise therefrom; now for the better encouraging, directing, and enabling the proprietors and undertakers, or others that are or may be concerned therein, their heirs and assigns, to manage, carry on, and improve said mines to the best advantage," etc.

The act authorized the appointment of three commissioners, William Pitkin, John Haynes, and John Hooker, who were to settle all controversies, and who were authorized to summon a jury in disputes exceeding forty shillings in amount. The sessions of this court were held generally at or near the mines, and great numbers of business and litigated cases, were adjusted in a summary and economical way, for the space of more than sixty years. During that whole period, the company of proprietors worked the mines, either themselves, or by leasing to other parties, who agreed to pay the company a percentage of the ore or metal produced. In their leases it was expressly stipulated, as follows:—

> "They also paying thereof to his Majesty, his heirs and successors, the fifth part of all gold and silver oar and precious stones, which from time to time, and at all times hereafter shall happen to be found, gotten, had and obtained within the aforesaid demised premises, or in any part or parcel thereof."

Thus acknowledging themselves most loyal subjects of taxation and revenue to the crown of England.

It is not ascertained what per cent. of profits was made on the investment in these mines, over and above the expenses of working them, but it is natural to suppose that if they were very profitable to the operators, all the applause usually attendant upon good luck, would not have remained forever hidden in oblivion from the world. Still the illusive charms of mining, had so much of novelty and hope for adventurers in the New World, that new companies were formed successively at various periods.

Some of the companies were composed of persons of great wealth and respectability. One company was formed in

London, one in Holland, others in Boston, New York, and elsewhere. In 1714, the records show that the use of the mines was purchased by Johnathan Belcher of Boston, (afterwards governor), Timothy Woodbridge Jr., and William Partrige; and in 1721 they had miners from Germany employed, and were expending seventy pounds a month in the work, It appears that this Boston company operated the mines for a period of at least twenty-three years, and in a letter from Governor Belcher, dated 1735, he states that he had disbursed upwards of fifteen thousand pounds, or about seventy-five thousand dollars.

In 1721 a division of the mining lands took place among the lessees, and each company worked at separate mines situated upon, and less than one mile from Copper Hill. At Higley's mine, about one and a half miles south, are now the remains of old workings which were operated at a later period than the others. At the breaking out of the War of the Revolution, Edmund Quincy of Boston had miners working at that place, but the works were soon after abandoned. After 1778 the old Copper Hill mines were deserted for fifty-three years, until a new company began operations in 1831.

The excitement in the colonies upon the business of mining, about that period, was very great, as it would seem from the following petition, copied from the records:

" *To the Honnell, the Gov'r Councill and Representatives in General Court assembled in New Haven, Oct. 16th A. D. 1733.*

"The Prayer of *Joseph Whiting*, of New Haven, Humbly Sheweth; That your Suppliant has expended a considerable time and money in Searching after Mines, and has made farther Discoveries perhaps than any other man in this Colony has before done. and having met with such incourgement as that I am willing to be at farther Expense in the Same Search—but ready money being so absolutely necessary therein; I therefore Humbly pray this assembly will be pleased to lease me one thousand pounds of the money Granted last may to be struck, and now to be disposed of by this assembly—upon double security in Lands and Bonds, for the payment of the interest every year; the principall to be Returned at the Expiration of ten years," &c. *Joseph Whiting.*"

A great deal of time and money without doubt was expended as the aforesaid petitioner says "*in searching after mines,*" for the evidence may be seen in the numerous pits and shafts which have been dug along the whole range of this mountain to New Haven. At that day, as in all previous time since the world began, and as is seen especially at the present day, the chief aim of many appeared to be to make fortunes by head-work—by speculation, and choosing rather to spend their time and risk their money in mining, and other uncertain projects—than to dig upon the *surface* of good old mother earth, for a sure and honest living.

Upon the summit of the hill where the greatest excavations were made, and the largest quantity of ore taken, two perpendicular shafts were dug principally through solid rock, for the purpose of raising the ore. One of them is nearly eighty feet deep, and the other thirty-five. At the bottom of these shafts we find the *caverns,* so termed, extending in various directions, several hundred feet. By estimating the once solid contents of these subterraneous vaults, an idea can be formed of the great quantity of ore which has been taken out. The percolation of water through the crevices of rock, made it necessary to dig drains or *levels* to convey it off; but these either became obstructed, or the mines were sunk below them, which allowed the accumulation of water, and it became necessary to discharge it by working the pumps day and night. This was done by employing the people in the vicinity and from neighboring towns, and from the amount expended for this service—three hundred and fifty dollars per month—it is believed that from twenty-five to thirty men were kept at work.

The copper ore has somewhat the appearance of yellowish grey sandstone, intermixed with nodules of bluish sulphuret, and yellow pyrites, and is very hard and brittle.

The vein is considered as rich, yielding ten to fifteen per cent. of pure copper, and some masses have been obtained yielding over forty per cent. The ore is of a character termed *refractory,* and the metal does not readily separate from the stone when pulverised and washed, in consequence of the specific gravity of the stony particles.

The mines would doubtless have been profitable to the operators at the price at which copper metal was at that time valued, had not the enterprise been shackled with various incumbrances. A principal one was, the laws of the mother country prohibiting the smelting of it here. The rigid laws of Britain imposed penalties upon any who should attempt to compete with her furnaces and artisans at home, consequently the vast expense of shipping it across the Atlantic, crippled the success of all parties engaged in the business. Notwithstanding the enormous expense, several cargoes were sent to Europe. A large quantity was deposited about one mile east of the mountain, in East Granby, upon a spot now marked by an entire dearth of vegetation, owing to the poisonous qualities extracted from the ore. From there it was carried fourteen miles to Hartford, where it was shipped to New York, and thence to England. The owners were still further disheartened by the loss of two vessels with their cargoes of ore. One was seized and confiscated as a prize by the French who were then at war with England; the other was sunk in the English Channel by shipwreck.

In defiance of British restrictions, considerable ore was smelted by the companies. Buildings and furnaces for pounding, smelting, and refining, were erected in Simsbury upon a stream of water called Hop Brook, a few miles distant, but safety required caution and secrecy in the works, which were for many years abandoned. The place where the smelting was carried on, was named by the German workmen, "Hanover," from their native place in Germany, which name it still retains. The mining-works at 'Hanover' were attached in 1725, and 1700 pounds of what was termed "black copper" (it not having been refined) was levied upon.

Granby Coppers.

Coin was made from this ore in 1737 and 1739, by a Mr. Higley, and was in current circulation for many years. In describing these coins, a writer says: They were stamped upon planchets of the purest copper, and, in consequence, were in demand by goldsmiths for alloy. The trade of a blacksmith, ever since Vulcan was engaged in forging thunderbolts, has given to the world some very remarkable men, and it affords us great pleasure at this time to be able to contribute to the fame of one of the craft, who not only devised, but manufactured currency. We have seen it stated that Mr. Higley, the author of these coppers, was an ingenious blacksmith who resided in the town of Granby; hence the name "Granby Coppers" and that with all the notions of utility which he naturally derived from the anvil, he was ambitious of making a little reputation for himself besides. He has certainly left evidence of having been an artist as well as financier, for the creations of his genius and skill were, for the times, well executed, and they also became a currency. Subsequently, we are informed, his cupidity led him into the hazardous experiment of illegally imitating the issues of other coiners, which, being discovered, deprived him of a portion of the laurels that had previously encircled his brow.* These coppers bear the symbols of their origin, with a due regard to royalty on some of them—the sledgehammers being surmounted by crowns, a something very apparent to the minds of the colonists, but which did not always command their sincere reverence. These coins grace but few cabinets, having been generally so impaired by wear, from being stamped upon unalloyed copper, as to be rarely found sufficiently perfect. We were, however, lately gratified by finding in New York city an electrotype which was perfect. Single specimens of this coin now command from fifteen to twenty-five dollars each. There appear to have

---

* The impression that Mr H. was a counterfeiter does not seem to be sustained by any recorded evidence. It is more probable, that owing, to the jealousy of England, which at that period crippled all such enterprises here, notice was served upon him that his embryo mint was regarded as an infringement upon the royal prerogatives, and he was for that reason obliged to suspend operations.

been five different issues of them, of several devices; upon one is the figure of a broad axe, with the motto "*I cut my way through.*"

The engraving represents both sides of a Granby copper,

now in the Connecticut Historical Society, at Hartford, from which the above cuts have been engraved for this work.

No public laws had been made by the colonists to authorize coinage of money, or to specify its value. Specie was very scarce in this country, and the coinage at this embryo mint, was regarded with great favor by the residents in the vicinity. The foreign trade of the country, which was chiefly confined to England, was principally controlled by her; the balance of trade was continually against us, which prevented the importation of specie. The war between England and France, in 1745, turned the tide somewhat in our favor, and considerable quantities were circulated in the colonies by England in payment of war expenses.

Owing to the scarcity of coin the colonists resorted to the use of Colonial Bills of Credit, the first issue of which was made by them in 1709, being the same year in which a public act was passed relating to the Simsbury mines. Previous to that time "Provision Pay" was the usual medium of exchange, consisting of the common eatables and other products of the country. The appraised value of such commodities at that time, may be shown by the following extract from the records of the town of Simsbury, stipulating the pay of their clergyman in 1688. They agreed to pay him fifty pounds per annum "in good current pay, to wit: one third in good merchantable wheat at four shillings per bushel, one third in pease or rye, at three shillings per bushel, and one third in Indian corn or pork; the corn at two shillings and six pence per bushel, and the pork at three pounds ten shillings per barrel," besides other items, fuel, &c. At an ordination nine years later, among the articles furnished on the occasion were the following, with their prices; "Half a lamb of mutton, 2s. 6d.; butter 6d. per pound; four pounds of sugar, 2s. 6d.; half a bushel Indian meal, 1s. 3d.; two fowls, 8d.; eighty-four pounds of beef, 15s.; thirty pounds venison, 3s. 9d.; nineteen pounds of pork, 4s. 9d.; nine pounds of mutton, 2s.; two gills of rum, 9d." Valued by our currency at this day the price of beef was three cents per pound; mutton three and a half cents, and venison two cents. In some instances it was stipulated that those who paid their rates in specie, should be allowed a discount of one third from the amount. Contracts between individuals unless specially stipulated to be paid in coin, were payable in the commodities of the neighborhood, and at prices established by the General Court. Taxes laid for military defence against the roving tribes of Indians, for building churches, and for ordinary public expenses, were also payable in produce. During a period of one hundred and forty eight years from the settlement of the colony to the peace of 1783, excepting the period of the French wars, the traffic among the people was carried on in part by barter and exchange. In 1709 it was enacted by the colony, that in order to assist in the expedition against the French in Canada, "there be forthwith imprinted a certain number of bills of credit, on the colony, in suitable sums from two shillings to five pounds, which in the whole shall amount to 8,000 pounds, and no more."

It was enacted that the bills should be received for dues and taxes, "at one shilling on the pound *better* than money." Taxes were imposed providing for the redemption of the whole amount within two years. The promptness with which the colony met their own bills, is noticeable when contrasted with the unavailing efforts of the Continental

Congress, to sustain the value of their paper money, which was issued in the Revolution.*

RECENT MINING.

The work at Simsbury mines was carried on at various periods until 1773, more than seventy years, through wars and rumors of wars, and by a variety of forces; by free labor, and by slave labor; by private enterprise, and by chartered companies; and, subsequently, by prison labor. Vast sums had been expended in the business, and then they were abandoned for the space of about half a century, for prison occupation.

In 1830, to the surprise of all, another resurrection of mineralogists was announced at the old prison mines. A company of gentlemen from New York, with Richard Bacon of Simsbury, formed the *Phœnix Mining Company*, obtained a charter, and purchased of the State the whole prison property, including the mines, and about five acres of land, for the sum of one thousand two hundred dollars. They expended many thousand dollars in digging extensive levels, building furnaces, and constructing engines and machinery, to facilitate their operations in raising, pounding, and smelting the ore. They carried on the business for some time, but owing to a reverse in the financial affairs of the country and other causes, the mines were again abandoned.

The old mines were suffered to repose again in quiet for about twenty years, when the note of preparation for working was once more heard. A new company was formed in 1855, called the *Connecticut Copper Company*, which prosecuted the business for about two years. They found the average

---

* To illustrate the ruinous depreciation of continental currency, I quote an extract from a letter written by *Hezekiah Munsell* of East Windsor. He says: "In 1781, in the months of Feb'y or March, I drove a team to Boston with a load, and brought one back for a merchant in Springfield, Mass. I had a five cattle team. Returning home I staid in Roxbury one night; my team was fed. I had one meal and lodging; my bill in the morning was two silver dollars, and continental money had so depreciated that I paid it in the round sum of $140 for that single night's entertainment."

yield of metal about ten per cent., and some masses of ore were taken out which produced over forty per cent. of copper. The deeper the descent, the richer appeared to be the quality of the ore. The chief obstacle to success appeared to be, not the lack of a fair percentage of metal, but in extracting it by the ordinary process of separating and fluxing; and for that purpose the company erected ten of Bradford's separators, at a great expense, and also two steam-engines for grinding, and for working the separating machines. The business has been suspended for about twenty years; but it is believed by many that with the aids of science, improved machinery, and sufficient capital, it may yet result profitably, and that Copper Hill may at no distant day, share some of the fame of the mines of Lake Superior.

The author has a specimen of pure copper extracted from the ore by Prof. Charles T. Jackson, formerly of Boston; also his process of analysis made in 1825, and sent to Hon. Samuel Woodruff, of East Granby, at his request.

"The Copper ore from East Granby, is composed of two distinct parts, the ore of a bright green color, which is the *Carbonate of Copper;* the other of a dark steel gray which is *Antimonial Gray Copper.* The specific gravity of the mass is 3.08.

ANALYSIS.

A. Two hundred grains, taken in equal quantities from each part of the specimen, were reduced to an impalpable powder and digested in a matrass repeatedly with two ounces of Nitro Muriatic Acid, until all the copper was dissolved; the silex remaining, after being well washed and ignited weighed 163 grains.

B. A pellicle which formed on the surface of the above solution proved to be sulphur, and weighed 4 grains.

C. The solution of copper etc., in Nitro Muriatic Acid was then evaporated to dryness and the dry mass again dissolved in concentrated Sulphuric Acid, the solution diluted and decanted, a white precipitate was observed at the bottom of the matrass which, when collected proved to be Sulph. Antimony which, on being decomposed gave 2 grains of Metallic Antimony.

D. The solution of copper in Sulphuric Acid was then poured into a proper vessel, and a polished cylinder of iron was introduced. In twelve hours the copper was precipitated in a metallic state around the cylinder. Collected, washed, and dried, the copper weighed 30 grains.

The enclosed slip of copper weighs 23 grains—7 grains having been lost in fusing it into a button and drawing it into this form.

CHARLES T. JACKSON."

From the preceding analysis it appears that the specimen yielded fifteen per cent. of pure copper.

Professors Silliman's Survey of the Mines.

A geological examination of Newgate Mines, was made by Prof. B. Silliman, four years ago, with a view to future working, and a report made to the Hon. Ezra Clark, the proprietor, from which the following extracts are made:—

"The vitreous copper is almost the only variety of ore of that locality, and is the only one of any economical importance. The yellow copper, the common Cornish ore, I have not seen here.

The composition of the vitreous ore in 100 parts is in round numbers, Copper 80, Sulphur 20. The variegated ore yields 69 parts copper in 100, and the yellow copper 32 parts in 100. It will be seen therefore that *the ore of your mine is one of the most valuable description.* The extent to which openings have been made north and south is about 800 feet, and from east to west from 250 to 300 feet. There are three parallel galleries from north to south, with numerous cross-cuts from east to west. These galleries have been made for the purpose of extracting the ore, but they embrace unbroken masses of the deposit which are now ready to be taken down by the miners. Of the extent of this deposit in *depth*, nothing can be known beyond the 250 to 300 feet now explored.

Result of the assay of three samples taken from the mines.

Best ore with seams of vitreous copper,	20.319 per cent.
Mottled ore in rusty sandstone,	14.370 " "
Granular rock with vitreous copper,	8.190 " "
Average of the samples,	14.029 " "

The average of the Cornish ores, England, is 7 to 8 per cent."

IMPRISONMENT OF THE TORIES.

Can then the verdure of these blissful plains
Conceal the *Caves* where penal Rigor reigns!
Where the starved wretch, by suffering folly led
To snatch the feast where pampered plenty fed;
Shut from the sunny breeze and healthful skies,
On the cold, dripping stone, low, withering, lies;
Torn from the clime that gave his visions birth,
A palsied member of the vital earth!
If the sweet Muse, with nature's best control,
Can melt to sympathy the reasoning soul,

> She bids thee rend those *grating bars* away,
> And o'er the dungeons break the beam of day:
> Give the frail felon with laborious toil,
> To pay the penance of his wasted spoil.
> Hear his deep groan, heed his repentant prayer,
> And snatch his frenzied spirit from despair;
> Nor let those fields, arrayed in heavenly bloom,
> Blush o'er the horrors of a *living tomb!**

These caverns were first occupied as a place for the confinement of Tories about the beginning of the American Revolution. What an astonishing train of events followed, and how distant from the thoughts of the British company of miners, the idea that they were actually hewing out prison cells, for the lodgement of their friends, the Tories of America!

The Colony of Connecticut first used the caverns as a permanent prison in 1773. A committee had been appointed by the general assembly to explore the place, who reported that by expending about thirty-seven pounds, the caverns could be so perfectly secured, that "it would be next to impossible for any person to escape." Whether their opinion was well founded, the reader may judge by the subsequent escapes, insurrections, and massacres which are recounted in the following pages. The total expense of purchasing the property, with the remaining lease of the mines, and fortifying the place, amounted to three hundred and seventy-five dollars.

An act was passed prescribing the terms of imprisonment. Burglary, robbery, and counterfeiting were punished for the first offence with imprisonment not exceeding ten years; second offence for life. The keeper of the prison was authorized to punish the convicts for offences, by "moderate whipping, not exceeding ten stripes, and by putting shackles and fetters upon them;" and it was intended to employ them at labor in the mines; which they did, to a considerable extent.

---

* Extract from a poem written by a lady of Boston, in 1797, after visiting the prison. It indicates the great notoriety and formidable character which **Newgate** had obtained, in the opinion of the benevolent and gifted poetess.

At first the number of Tories confined in the caverns did not exceed five or six, and these were guilty of various crimes against the government. But as time developed events, the numbers increased to between thirty and forty.

When the three hundred and forty-two chests of tea were thrown into the sea at Boston, in 1773, and that port closed by an Act of Parliament, so great was the excitement, and so indignant were the people, particularly in Massachusetts and Connecticut, on account of British oppression, that the use of tea and all commodities imported in British vessels and subject to duty, was prohibited. The duty on tea was so particularly obnoxious, that it was considered a contraband article of household comfort. True, the contrast in the times may appear rather curious, for at this day, a housekeeper would be judged by common consent deserving incarceration in the mines, or some other place, for *not* allowing the article to be used. Our ancestors knew no half-way policy, and seldom adopted dilatory measures to carry their points. Tea-vessels, if then kept at all, were kept out of sight; tea-pots were run into musket-balls, and they were the kind of currency with which the people dealt with old England.

The following incident from Dr. Stiles's History of Ancient Windsor, shows the marked spirit of the times:

"At an early period in the Revolutionary struggle, and before the war had fairly commenced, some of the Tories (of whom there were a few in Windsor) happened one day to come across *Elihu Drake*, then a lad about eight years old, and partly in earnest, and partly in a joke, endeavored to compel him to say, *God save the King*. Failing of success, they tried to intimidate him by threatening him with a ducking in the river. But the boy still stoutly refused. Becoming somewhat enraged at the young rebel, they carried their threat into execution, and thrust him under water, but as they pulled him out spluttering and choking, the only exclamation which he uttered was a fervent *God d—n the King*. Again, and again was the little martyr thrust under, but each time the same reply was all they could extort from him, and they were obliged to release him with many hearty curses for his stubbornness. At the age of twelve, this young hero accompanied his father into the war, in the capacity of waiter."

The following from the Connecticut Journal, in 1775, further illustrates the spirit of animosity against the Tories:

"The Riflemen on their way from the Southern colonies through the country, administer the new-fashioned discipline of tar and feathers to the obstinate and refractory *Tories* that they meet on their road, which has had a very good effect here (in New Milford). Those whose crimes are of a more atrocious nature, they punish by sending them to Gen. Gage. They took a man in this town, a most incorrigible Tory, who called them d——d rebels, &c., and made him walk before them to Litchfield, which is 20 miles, and carry one of his own geese all the way in his hand; when they arrived there, they tarred him, and made him pluck his goose, and then bestowed the feathers on him, drummed him out of the company, and obliged him to kneel down and thank them for their lenity."

Public opinion in some of the colonies against those who favored the mother country was very rigid, authorizing any person even to shoot them if they were found beyond the limits of their own premises, and one was shot in the town of Simsbury, another was hung publicly in Hartford and the gallows was left standing for some time to intimidate other Tories. Those who possessed not the hardihood thus summarily to dispatch a neighbor when he declined to fight for the country, or for purchasing foreign goods, adopted the more humane expedient of applying to the Committee of Safety* in the town, who penned them up in the caverns where they could at least leisurely examine the evidence of British labor, though not allowed the blessed boon of being governed by British laws. The following extract is from the biography of the celebrated Bishop Griswold :—

"As an instance of the manner in which not only the clergy but others of the church were watched, I will here insert the account given me on my visit to Simsbury, of the proceedings against Bishop Griswold's father. For a time this worthy man was arraigned almost daily before the Committee of Vigilance, and straightly questioned as to the most common actions of his life; but as nothing was actually found against him, the committee contented themselves with forbidding him to go beyond the limits of his own farm. This, however, as his farm was something of a little terrritory, gave him space for exercise, particularly as he was a home-keeping man, and seldom left his farm save of a Sunday for church.

*In some towns they were termed Committee of Inspection. They constituted what we should call a Committee of Vigilance, and their duties were of a very peculiar and delicate nature—"a patriotic and searching *espionage* into the principles, actions, and private affairs of every member of the community, without regard to station, profession, or character. It was

His uncle (Rev. Roger Viets), however, being a public man and more closely associated in public opinion with the interests of the royal cause, was not only more closely watched, but also more rigorously treated. He was naturally of a very kind and charitable disposition, and to the suffering was ever ready to extend relief. It happened that, at midnight one time, some men who it afterwards appeared were endeavoring to elude pursuit, called at his house and asked for charitable aid. Lodging he dared not give them. Food he could not refuse. Of this charitable deed some circumstances led the authorities into a suspicion, and being accused of it he would not deny what he had done; and for that act of benevolence, which, as he believed, the law of God required, he was condemned to be imprisoned, and was many months confined in jail at Hartford."

We cannot for a moment doubt the noble intentions of the American patriots in the severity of those measures, for the results are now universally acknowledged, and generally appreciated. If at the commencement of their struggles for liberty, they had permitted those emmissaries to raise a question as to the right of independent government, and had suffered them to prowl about unmolested, spreading the fuel of disaffection, a *civil*, instead of a national war must have followed. The proud eagle of Liberty would not so soon have risen over this land of plenty, and the *reveille* of British soldiery would have told misfortune's tale,—a government of force. Well would it be for us their descendants if like them we could appreciate the blessings of liberty, of our happy form of government, and the value of mutual peace and union of this great confederacy of States!

---

necessary to know how each man stood affected towards the war—whether his feelings were enlisted in his country's behalf, or whether secretly or publicly he was aiding the enemy." If any individual fell under suspicion of *the people*, the committee were immediately notified, and they forthwith repaired to the person and demanded an avowal of his sentiments. If found to be lukewarm or indifferent to the liberal cause, he was closely watched. If a Tory in sentiment, he was remanded to Newgate. The dividing line of principle was positive and distinct. On the royal side, the British officials proclaimed those to be outlaws who favored the cause of the *rebels*, and pronounced free pardon to such as ceased their resistance, or espoused the cause of Royalty. Besides this it is said they gave secret protection-papers to those applying for them on the score of friendship. These acts of the British impelled the colonist to take the most rigorous measures in self-defense.

At this day, it seems to us hardly possible that any considerable number could have been found so indifferent to the possession of liberty as to oppose their countrymen in arms, struggling for freedom, and the inalienable rights of man. We are prone to regard them as inhuman, deluded beings, unworthy to live. But let us pause a moment, yield a little to our charity, and consider the state of the country at that time, and some of the influences by which they were surrounded. The Tories were aware that in the history of the world, every people who had attempted the experiment of a free representative form of government, although in some cases for a while successful, yet in the end had most positively failed in their hopes and plans; their struggles had only ended in loss of power by the many, and usurpation of it by the few. From the history of the Republics of Greece in early Europe, through the long vista of twenty-four centuries, the plebeian people had striven through toil and blood, only to bend their necks at last to the yoke of some powerful chieftain in war. The colonists and their ancestors had suffered and bled in the Indian wars, afterwards in wars with the French, and with French and Indians combined; and their mother England had been an ally who had assisted them in their defence, and to whom they still looked for aid in emergency. Many also, were bound by the ties of near kindred to friends across the ocean. Those in civil power received their authority direct from England, and many of the clergy were commissioned by the Church of England, from which also they received their chief support. All of them, doubtless, were inclined by early education and prejudice, to prefer a kingly to a republican government, and they dreaded the troublesome responsibility of beginning the contest for a change, well knowing that an ignominious death awaited them in case their experiment failed. In the words of our Declaration of Independence, "all experience hath shown that mankind are more disposed to suffer, while evils are sufferable, than to right themselves by abolishing the forms to which they are accustomed."

On the other hand, they are censurable for opposing independence, because the oppression of British tyranny had planted them or their fathers upon the inhospitable shores of a new world. They had generously expended their blood and treasure for the maintenance of the Crown, and had obeyed its mandates by assisting in the war against France, which resulted in the acquisition of a vast territory to the English nation. Their trade had been monopolized by her; then, when prudence would have dictated a relaxation of authority, the mother country rose in her demands, and imposed heavy taxes to pay off a national debt of more than $700,000,000. The idea should have been discarded, that a small island, more than two thousand miles distant, should hold in bondage, without representation, a territory on this continent, large as the whole of Europe, and destined to equal it in population. They should have remembered too, that citizens of the early Republics, possessed not our advantage of historical experience of other Republics, to point out the faults of free government by which they could avoid their errors, and adopt their benefits; and no well-defined system of confederated states, with a constitution limiting the just powers of government, had ever been devised. The masses in early ages were ignorant, superstitious, and heathenish; they were crammed into dense cities and villages, which are the hot-beds of vice and corruption; while on the contrary, the inhabitants of America could glean wisdom from the history of past ages, and commune with the great and mighty dead. They possessed abundance of territory for all; plenty of room in which to develop their free energies, and afford to all uneasy spirits a medium in which to expend their surplus gas, in the moral atmosphere of a continent. They could realize the sentiment:

> "No pent up Utica contracts our powers,
> For the whole boundless Continent is ours."

A writer says:—

"Of the Tories who engaged actively in the war against American independence, their subsequent history was for the most part a melancholy one. Probably not more than half of those who fled the country ever returned, and those who did were mostly broken-down men reduced to poverty, laden with the odium of having made war upon their country, and in many cases stained with vice and adicted to habits which sent them to an early grave. It was one of the questions which most impeded the negotiations for peace between the States and Great Britain in 1783,— What should be done with these Tories. Several thousand had removed to Canada, New Brunswick, and Nova Scotia, and most of whom were in circumstances of extreme destitution. It was, at first insisted by the British negotiators, that Congress should grant pardon to all political offenders of this sort, restore their confiscated estates, and remunerate them for the losses they had suffered. This was refused, on the ground: First; that Congress only had authority under the articles of Confederation to *recommend* measures to the several States. Secondly; that these men had encouraged the British to prosecute the war, and many of them had personally engaged in plundering and ravaging the country, and ought rather to be made to render compensation, than to receive it. Thirdly; that the the confiscated estates of the Tories had been sold and re-sold, often divided and could not now be restored without endless litigation. And finally, that in the impoverished condition of the country, it was impossible to pay its own meritorious soldiers. The matter was finally compromised by inserting three articles into the treaty, to the effect that the loyalists (or Tories) should not be debarred from collecting debts due them before the war; that Congress would recommend to the States to restore confiscated property *as far as possible*, and that no future confiscations should be made or prosecutions begun. These terms were at length reluctantly agreed to by Great Britain,

The recommendations of Congress to the States were, however, ineffectual, as it was *probably expected* they would be.

Connecticut would not consent to restore the property of such as has been engaged in burning Danbury, Fairfield, and other sea-coast towns. The same was true in other states, Let England, they said, pay us for the wanton injuries she has inflicted, before she asks compensation, for the traitors by whom it was done. Failing thus in securing relief from the States for her refugees, Parliament undertook the duty for themselves. A commissioner was appointed by England to ascertain the losses incurred by their friends, and about fifteen and a half million dollars was appropriated for their compensation."

Besides this, many of the loyalists of America received subsidies and pensions from the British government during their lives, some received large grants of lands, and some half-pay as military officers.

The First Keeper of Newgate

was Capt. John Viets, who resided near by, and who supplied

them daily with such food and necessaries as were required. His bill, as recorded for one year, in 1774, is as follows:

"Captain *John Viets*, Master, as per his bill for services, boarding workmen and providing for prisoners, &c., 29*l*. 5*s*. 10*d*."

At that time no guard was kept through the day, but two or three sentinels kept watch during the night. There was an anteroom or passage, through which to pass before reaching their cell, and the usual practice of Capt. Viets, when he carried their food, was, to look through the gates into this passage, to observe whether they were near the door, and if not, to enter, lock the door after him, and pass on to the next. The inmates soon learned his custom, and accordingly prepared themselves for an escape. When the captain came next time, some of them had contrived to unbar their cell door, and huddled themselves in a corner behind the door in the passage, where they could not easily be seen, and upon his opening it, they sprang upon him, knocked him down, pulled him in, and taking the key from his possession, they locked him up and made good their escape. What were the captain's reflections on his sudden transition from keeper to that of prisoner is not stated, but he probably thought, with Falstaff, "discretion is the better part of valor," and that he must adopt, in future, more prudent measures. His absence was soon perceived by his family, who came to his relief. The inhabitants around rallied immediately, and gave chase to the absconding heroes, and finally succeeded in capturing nearly the whole of them. Several were taken in attempting to cross the Tunxis or Farmington River, at Scotland Bridge, a few miles south; sentinels having been stationed at that place to intercept them. Some—Santa Anna like—took refuge upon trees, and there met with certain capture. An aged and respected matron, then a child and residing but a few rods from the prison said to the author that, "the news of their escape and capture spread as much terror among the children in the neighborhood as if they had been a band of midnight assassins."

Although the prison was considered impregnable, the first

convict which had been put there, John Hinson, had escaped. He was committed, Dec. 2d, 1773, and escaped after a confinement of eighteen days, by being drawn up through the mining shaft, assisted, it is said, by a woman to whom he was paying his addresses. On the 26th of Feb. 1774, three prisoners were received; one of them escaped on the 9th of April following, and the two others on the 23d. One committed on the 5th of April took sudden leave on the 9th, having been confined just *four days!*

After the general escape and recapture, the following report was made by the overseers:

To the Honorable General Assembly now sitting at Hartford:

"We, the subscribers, overseers of Newgate Prison, would inform your Honors, that Newgate Prison is so strong and secure that we believe it is not possible for any person put there to escape, unless by assistance from abroad; yet it so happens that one *John Hinson*, lately sent there by order of the Honorable the Superior Court, has escaped by the help of some evil minded person at present unknown, who, in the night season next after the 9th inst., drew the prisoner out of the shaft; and we believe no place ever was or can be made so secure but that if persons abroad can have free access to such prison, standing at a distance from any dwelling house, the prisoners will escape; we therefore recommend it to your Honors, that some further security be added to that prison in order to secure the prisoners: what that security shall be, will be left to your Honors; yet we would observe to your Honors that the east shaft where the prisoner escaped, is about 70 feet to the bottom of the prison, the whole of which is through a firm rock, except 10 feet at top, which is stoned up like a well; we therefore propose that the upper part down to the rock be lock'd up, and stones about 15 or 18 inches square and of suitable length, be laid across said shaft about eight inches asunder &c. And as to the west shaft, which is about 25 feet deep, secured with a strong iron gate, about six feet below the surface, we propose that a strong log house be built of two or three rooms, one of which, to stand over this shaft to secure it from persons abroad, and the other rooms to be for the miners, &c. All which is submitted by your Honor's most obedient Humble Servants."

Erastus Wolcott,
Josiah Bissell,
Joh'n Humphrey.

Hartford Jan'y 17th 1774.

Connecticut at that period held each year two sessions of her Assembly, and at the next session, four months after, the following report was presented by the overseers:

To the Hon. the Gen'l Assembly now sitting at Hartford:

"We the subscribers hereto, overseers of Newgate Prison, beg leave to represent to your honors, That soon after the rising of the assembly in Jan'y last, three delinquents were committed from Windham, and two others from New London county, whereupon, notwithstanding the severity of the season, we immediately set about making those further securities that your Honours directed, and have built a strong log house 36 feet in length and 20 feet in width, with timbers 10 inches square, divided into two rooms, one of which includes the west shaft, and in the other, which is designed for the miners to lodge in, &c., we have built a chimney, and compleated the whole except the under floor, the planks for which are not yet sufficiently dryed and fit to lay, and some ceiling to secure the miners from the cold winds, which otherwise will pass betwixt the timbers. We have also secured the east shaft where the first prisoner escaped, with iron and stone, and every other place where we thought it possible for any to escape; and we apprehend that said prison is now well secured and fitted to receive and employ those offenders that may be sent there. An account of our disbursements, &c., we have ready to lay before your Honours or Auditors, to be appointed as your Honours shall direct. Your Honours must have heard that the prisoners have all escaped that prison; it would be long, and perhaps difficult, in writing, to give a particular and distinct account how this was done; your Honours will excuse us if we only say that they effected their escape by the help of evil minded persons abroad, before the necessary and proposed securityes could be compleated. We would further inform your Honours, that we had engaged two miners to assist the prisoners at work, who were to have been there about the time the prisoners escaped, and one of them actually left his business and came there a few days after the escape; him we have retained, and to this time principally employed in compleating the securities to the prison; the other we gave intelligence of the escape before he left his business, and prevented his coming; but have engaged him to attend when wanted. All which is submitted to your Honours, by your Honours' most obedient and humble servants."

Hartford, May 14th, 1774.

ANOTHER ESCAPE

was attempted by the prisoners, in 1776, by burning the block-house over the shaft. A level had been opened from the bottom of the mines through the hill westward, for the purpose of draining off the water, and the mouth of this level was closed by a heavy wooden door firmly fastened. They had by degrees collected sufficient combustibles, and with a piece of stone and steel they kindled a fire against the door, which burned as well as damp fuel in a damp dungeon naturally would; but instead of making their escape from the prison, they all nearly made their final escape from the world; for the dense smoke and blue flame soon filled the apartment and almost suffocated all of them. Search being made, one of them was found dead, and five others were brought forth senseless, but finally recovered.

They were afterwards placed in a strong wooden building, erected for the purpose above ground, in 1777. They set this building on fire the next year, and burned it to the ground. Nearly all escaped, but several of them were afterwards retaken.

In 1780, the block-house, so called, was rebuilt; but prudence by the officers in the management was disregarded. Had they been more careful in adopting safeguards for themselves and the prisoners, they might have avoided the dreadful scene which was soon to follow—

A Scene of Conflict and Blood!

It appears that the overseers relied for security upon the number of guards rather than upon their proper discipline, as they appointed a lieutenant, one sergeant, one corporal and twenty-four privates, while the number of prisoners was only thirty—thus providing the very liberal complement of about one soldier to each prisoner. The guards were armed with loaded muskets and fixed bayonets, and the officers with cutlasses and pistols.

As the war with England now raged with fury, the animosity between the Whigs and Tories had grown in proportion, and the seal of distinct party was in many places stamped with vivid impression, so that at this period the number doomed to the prison had amounted to thirty, and many of them were Tories. They were a desperate set of men and scrupled at no means of escape. On the night of the 18th of May, 1781, the dreadful tragedy occurred which resulted in the escape of all the prisoners. A prisoner was confined, by the name of Young, and his wife wishing to be admitted into the cavern with him, she was searched, and while two officers were in the act of raising the hatch to let her down, the prisoners rushed out, knocked down the two officers, and seizing the muskets of nearly all the rest who were asleep, immediately took possession of the works, and thrust most of the guards into the dungeon, after a violent contest. One of them, Mr. Gad Sheldon, was mortally wounded, fighting at his post, and six more wounded severely. Said a venerable old lady now deceased: "It was a dreadful sight to see the wounded guards, as they were brought into our house one after another, and laid upon the floor, weltering in their blood! When I came into the room, the faithful Sheldon sat on a bench, his body bent forward, and a bayonet dripping with blood lying before him, which he had just drawn out of his breast—it was a deadly stab!" Many of the prisoners were wounded; some of them were assailed and gashed by their comrades through mistake, while fighting in the darkness of the conflict. Nearly all made their escape; some from their wounds were unable to flee. One was taken on a tree in Turkey Hills, east of the mountain; and a few others were found in swamps and barns in the neighboring towns.

The foregoing is corroborated by a paper just received, as this work was going to press. It is copied from Rivington's "*Gazetteer*," a Tory weekly paper printed in New York, in 1773. In Nov. 1775, the paper was mobbed by a party of Connecticut men, but when the British gained possession of that city, in 1777, the paper was revived. Rivington styled himself "Printer to the King."

It appears by the following statement that the men were tory privateers, who had been commissioned by the British to plunder the Connecticut towns on the borders of L. I. Sound. It says:—

"June 6th, 1781.—This day arrived in New York, Ebenezer Hathaway and Thomas Smith, who on the 16th of May last made their escape from Simsbury Mines after a most gallant struggle for their liberty. These men declare that they were two of eight belonging to the privateer boat Aventure which was duly commissioned; that they were taken in Huntington Bay, Long Island, on the 7th of April by seven rebel whale-boats manned with seventy-three men, and that night carried across the Sound to Stamford, in Connecticut; that the next day they were carried to what they called headquarters, before Gen. Waterbury, who, with the air of a demagogue ordered them to Hartford Gaol, and told the guard they had his liberty to strip them even to the clothes remaining on their backs; but the captors had left them so bare that all they had about them now was not an object even to a Yankee soldier; there they lay until the 27th following when their trial came on before the superior court; that they were brought before the court and directed to plead not guilty and offered for counsel Colonel Sention, one of the justices, then on the bench, in order that they might by law bring them in guilty; but aware of their knavish tricks, they declared themselves British subjects and refused to plead either guilty or not guilty, therefore they were ordered to Newgate Gaol, or rather to that inquisition, Simsbury Mines, which from the following description exceed anything among their allies in France or Spain.

These poor unfortunate victims, relate that they were taken from Hartford Gaol and marched under a strong guard to Simsbury Mines distant about *seventy-four* miles. In approaching this horrid dungeon they were first conducted through the apartments of the guards, then through a trap-door downstairs into another upon the same floor with the kitchen, which was divided from it by a very strong partition door. In the corner of this outer room, and near the foot of the stairs, opened another large trap-door, covered with bars and bolts of iron, which was hoisted up in two guards by means of a tackle, whilst the hinges grated as they turned upon their hooks, and opened the jaws and mouth of what they call Hell, into which they descended by means of a ladder about six feet more, which led to a large iron grate or hatchway, locked down over a shaft of about three feet diameter, sunk through the solid rock, and which they were told led to the bottomless pit. Finding it not possible to evade this hard, cruel fate they bade adieu to the world and descended the ladder about thirty-eight feet more, when they came to what is called the landing; then marching shelf by shelf till descending about thirty or forty feet more they came to a platform of boards laid under foot, with a few more put overhead to carry off the water which keeps continually dropping. Here, say they, we found the inhabitants of this woful mansion who were exceedingly anxious to know what was going on above. We told them that Lord Cornwallis had beat the rebel army and that their money was gone to the d——l, with which they seemed satisfied and rejoiced at the good news.

They were obliged to make use of pots of charcoal to dispel the foul air, which in some degree is drawn off by the means of a ventilator or auger hole which is bored from the surface through at this spot, said to be seventy feet perpendicular. Here they continued twenty days and nights, resolved, however, to avail themselves of the first opportunity to get out, although they should lose their lives in the attempt. Accordingly on the 18th, eighteen of them being let up to the kitchen to cook, found means to break the lock of the door which kept them from the foot of the ladder leading to the guard-room. They now doubly resolved to make a push should the door be opened; which fortunately was the case about ten o'clock at night, (to let down a prisoner's wife who had come there and was permitted to see him.)

Immediately they seized the fortunate moment and rushed up, but before any, except one, got out, the door was slammed down on the rest, and he, the brave Captain Hathaway, who commanded the adventure, scuffled with the whole of them for a few minutes and was wounded in three different places when he was nobly assisted by his trusty friend, Thomas Smith, and afterwards by the other eight. They then advanced upon the guard consisting of twenty-four in number, and took the whole prisoners. This was no sooner accomplished than they brought their companions out of the bottomless pit and put the guard down into their room, then marched off with their arms and ammunition, but were soon afterwards obliged to disperse."

A Committee was appointed by the Assembly, then in session, to repair to Newgate and inquire into the facts respecting the insurrection. They reported the evidence in the case, some of which it is curious to notice in their own words, as follows:—

"*Jacob Southwell* was awakened by the tumult, took a gun and run out of the guard-house, and durst not go back for fear they would hurt him. N. B. A young man *more fit to carry fish to market*, than to keep guard at Newgate. *Nathan Phelps* was also asleep—wak'd but could do nothing, the prisoners having possession of the guard-house (a small lad just fit to drive plow with a very gentle team.) He went to Mr. *Viets's* and stayed till morning (poor boy)! *Abagail*, the wife of *Jno. Young*, *alias Mattick*, says that the first night she came to prison, she gave to her husband 52 silver dollars—her husband told her after he came out that he had given Sergt. *Lilly* 50 of them in order that he may suffer the prisoners to escape—that he told her the Sergt. purposely left the door of the south jail unlocked—that Sergt. *Lilly* was not hurt—that she borrowed the money of a pedler—that she heard *Lilly* say, it was a great pity such likely men should live and die in that place."

Nov. 6th, 1782, the wooden buildings of the prison were again destroyed by fire, and doubtless by design, in order to aid the escape of the Tories in confinement. This was the *third* time the prison buildings had been burned in nine years, since its first inauguration, and more than one-half of the whole number of convicts had escaped by various means. The authorities probably by this time began to change their opinion that "it would be next to impossible for any person to escape," and that as a Yankee once said, it was "dangerous being safe."

The following is too rich in orthography to be omitted. It is recorded as written in 1783:

To the Hon. General Assembly, The humble petishen of *Able Davis*—whare as at the honerable supene court houlden in Hartford in December last I was conficted of mis Deminer on the count of newgate being burnt as I had comand of said gard and was orded to bee confind 3 month and pay fourteen pounds for disabaing orders, I cant read riten, but I did all in my power to distingus the flame, but being very much frited and not the faculty to doe as much in distress as I could another time and that is very smaul, what to do I thot it was best to let out the prisners that war in the botams as I had but just time to get the gates lifted before the hous was in flames, and the gard bein frited it twant in my power to scape them. I now pray to be Deflehaned from further in prisment, and the coust of said sute as I hante abel to pay the coust, or give me the liberty of the yard as I am very unwell as your pitishner in duty bound wi l for ever pray. *Abel Daveis.*
Hartford Goal, January 14th, 1783.

The struggles at this prison to subdue Toryism, were doubtless greater than at any other place in any of the Colonies. Many of those in confinement were men of talents, spirit, and wit; and they occasionally indulged their proclivities by making poetry in derision of the measures which were carried on by the patriots against England. The following is a part of some rhymes (referring to the patriots) composed by them, and sent to their keeper:

"Many of them in halters will swing,
Before *John Hancock* will ever be king."

John Hancock, being one of the most ardent friends of the Revolution, was particularly obnoxious to the British, and a price was set on his head; this raised the spirit of the colonists, and they at once elected him President of Congress, which drew upon him the special odium of the Tories.

The following is from the original now in the possession of the author:

"Mr. *Viets:* If you have any *meet* cooked, you will much *oblidge* me by sending a dinner, for I suffer for want. "*Peter Sackett.*"

This man was one of the thirty who were engaged in a bloody contest with the guard, and he made his escape at that time. The imprisoned Tories were not without sympathizers, and spiritual comforters. The Rev'd Roger Viets, an Episcopal clergyman, a resident of Simsbury, and previously alluded to, occasionally expounded the gospel to them, and taught them the gospel precept, "Honor the King." His reverence was a noted good liver among the people, and besides what was given him in donations, he received annually forty pounds from the established Church of England. After Independence was acknowledged by Great Britain, the salaries of the clergy were discontinued, but the Church "Propagation Society" of England offered to continue the stipends to such of the American Clergy, as would remove to the British dominions where parishes were assigned them. Mr. Viets among others, considered it prudent to accept the offer, and emigrated to Nova Scotia, where his descendants now reside in respectable circumstances.

A Tory Clergyman in Newgate.

The choicest specimen of black-hearted treason under the cloak of priestly sanctity, was exhibited in the person of a Tory of the name of Simeon Baxter, who was confined in the caverns. From which of the thirteen colonies he was sent, is not ascertained, but he must have been regarded by the people as a real champion of Toryism. He preached a sermon to his companions in prison, in 1781, which was printed in London soon after. On account of its novelty of conception, acrimony of spirit, ability, and pungency, it is here published entire, with its title in full, as it was printed. It will be observed that the text, as he quotes it, varies from the precise phraseology of the scriptures; the words "having descended" being surreptitiously employed, probably because he considered them an improvement on the scriptures as applicable to his situation, he being compelled to descend into the caverns. Whatever may be thought of his sentiments, the ability with which the discourse was written proves its author to have been a man of powerful intellect and of considerable research, zealously determined to incite his companions to deeds of blood. It is indeed wonderful that Gen. Washington or the Continental Congress escaped assassination, when such vindictive characters boldly advised a resort to the dagger in order to exterminate the friends of liberty.

"*Tyrannicide proved Lawful, from the Practice and Writings of Jews, Heathens, and Christians: A Discourse, delivered in the Mines at Symsbury, in the Colony of Connecticut, to the Loyalists confined there by Order of the Congress, on September 19, 1781, by* SIMEON BAXTER, *a Licentiate in Divinity, and voluntary Chaplain to those Prisoners in the Apartment called Orcus:*

Having descended, he preached to the Spirits in Prison.—1st Peter, iii, 19. *Regnabit sanguine multo—ad Regnum quisquis venit ab Exilo.* Whoever comes to his kingdom from exile, he will rule with much blood.— *Suetonius's life of Nero.*

Printed in America; London, Reprinted for S. Blandon in Pater-Noster Row, MDCCLXXXII."

" *To General Washington, and the Congress styling themselves Governors and Protectors of Thirteen Colonies belonging to the Crown of England:*

"Gentlemen, That you may have the honour of dying for the people, instead of their dying for you and your allies, was the design I had in preaching and publishing this discourse; and should it produce the desired effect, I shall think myself paid for all my trouble and expence. If you can bestow one generous deed on your ruined country, adopt the act of *Suicide* to balance the evils of your lives, and save the virtuous citizens of America the glorious trouble of doing justice on you.

"Remember Judas was not a patriot till he hanged himself for betraying his Saviour and his God. *Go thou and do likewise* and you will prove yourselves real Saviours of America, and like him, hold a place in the temple of everlasting Fame. Should your courage or your virtue fail in so meritorious a deed, sacred Religion stands on tiptoe to inspire all her children by some hidden thunder or some burnished weapon, to do it for you, and to save themselves from Nimrod's paradise. When you are dead, your grateful countrymen will not let your Honours lie in dust, but will raise you to some airy tomb between the drooping clouds and parching sands: then your exaltation will make islands glad; Peace with new-fledged wing, shall fly through every state, and echo happiness to weeping willows; nay, the mourning doves shall forsake the wilderness to chant your praises; and the mope-eyed owls, in open day, shall view with wonder your patriotic virtues. *The Author.*"

"*To the Protestant Rebel Ministers of the Gospel in the Thirteen Confederated Colonies in America:*

" Gentlemen—The bloody part you have acted in obedience to your creditors, the merchants smugglers, both in the pulpit and the field, with your spiritual and temporal swords, entitles you to the second class of patriots, who disgrace religion with hypocrisy, and humanity with barbarity. Spectators with great justice have decided, that you are the successors of him who went to and fro seeking whom he might devour, and not of him who went about doing good. Inasmuch as you began rebellion because your King would not persecute, but tolerate his faithful catholic subjects in

Canada, and to support your rebellion, you have since joined yourselves unto idols, and made alliance with the Papists of France to root up the protestant religion,* for which our fathers bled and died, inasmuch as you have out-acted the Pope, discarded and abjured your rightful king, neglected to visit those in prison, and forbid the exercise of that charity to the miserable, which hides a multitude of sins, I must take leave of you in the words spoken to your predecessors by the Saviour of all penitent sinners, 'Go your way for I know you not.' *The Author.*"

SERMON.

Then three men of Judah went to the top of the rock Etam, and said to Samson, knowest thou not that the Philistines are rulers over us? and what is this that thou hast done unto us? And he said unto them: As they did unto me, so have I done unto them.—*Judges* xv. 11.

"In the beginning of this chapter we are told that the children of Israel again did evil in the sight of the Lord, for which they were delivered into the hands of the Philistines forty years; a heavy judgment to fall under the power of any people without law, justice, or mercy! yet God has considered such a calamity as due to idolaters, and the enemies of common sense. Whatever nation is governed by a set of men like the Philistines, without any fixed rules of right, is controlled by a set of beasts, with sharp horns, arrogance, and pride. Israel being thus in bondage, God raised up Samson to deliver them, who went down to Timnath, and took a wife of the Philistines, of whom he was unjustly robbed, without hopes of any legal redress. After this outrage, Samson had a just opportunity to make war upon them, which he did, though unassisted and opposed by his servile countrymen. The men of Judah, like modern politicians, were alarmed at the war which threatened them, and sought peace with the Philistines by joining against their deliverer, and accosted him in the words of the text. "What is this that thou hast done unto us?" Samson answered, and justified his conduct upon the law of nature: "As they have done unto me so have I done unto them,"—a good defence against the Philistines, who acted upon private principles, and trampled under foot the laws of God and civil society. Had the case been otherwise, Samson, who judged Israel twenty years, and whom the Lord blessed, would have sought justice from the decision of an impartial judge, instead of redressing himself by the natural law of retaliation. There are but two ways of deciding differences; the one is by law, the other by force. The first is the rule of men formed into civil societies; the second of men and beasts in the state of nature.

Kings of civil societies, in a just war, have recourse to the state of nature, and use their last arguments, when justice cannot be had for injuries received. Cicero, one of the luminaries of the heathen world, asserts that "war is supported by us against those of whom we can obtain no law." Grotius, the great oracle of Christians, saith that "the law forbids me to pursue my right but by a course of law." This is a good law in civil society,

---

* He probably refers to our treaty of alliance made with France.

where justice is administered according to the laws of right, where the innocent are protected against oppressors; but in a state of nature, where no law but that of power doth exist, the maxim of Grotius is not applicable, unless the nature of law is to support the tyrants, and oppress the afflicted.

Moses, the legislator of the Jews, knowing that men were partial to themselves, unjust to others, and unfit to be their own judges, ordered their controversies to be decided according to the law: but whilst Israel was in Egypt, law and justice had no place; whereupon Moses, to point out the law of nature, set an example to be followed by all men on proper occasions; he saw his brethren oppressed, an Egyptian smiting an Hebrew, and knowing he could obtain no legal satisfaction, erected an high court of justice, and smote the Egyptian, which proves we may revert to the law of nature, and repel force by force, and do justice for ourselves when no legal justice can be had. If this be not the case, law is a scourge to the oppressed, and a protection to tyrants, which is contrary to the spirit of all laws, which always provide remedies for slaves against their cruel masters. Since the law of God and man takes care for slaves, and protects them from the injuries of their masters, how unreasonable is it, that the free people of America, who have only God for their master, should find no redress against the oppressions of a barbarous set of usurpers and tyrants, who have laid waste our once happy country, and murdered our friends and relations before our eyes; who, to calm our complaints of misery, either hang us upon trees, or cast us into some darksome prison, where their midnight assassins launch us out of time. Merciful God! if our wives and children have the privilege of starving in the streets, we are taught to reverence the favor as an act of lenity in Congress and its associates!

Since we live in an evil time, when all laws of civil society are repealed, "the whole head sick and heart faint," the people crouching beneath their burdens and crying, "let us alone that we may serve the Egyptians," while the Levites from their pulpits, like the men of Judah from the top of Etam, are proclaiming "know you not that the Congress are rulers over us? and is it not better to serve them than to die by the hand of Saul or the bitter water of Marah?" Since this is not the voice of wisdom, but of Athalia, of Mattan and his priests who were slain at the horse-gate and the altar, according to the law of retaliation, let us return to our natural right, and act the magistrate upon those usurpers who have shut up the course of justice. For our encouragement we have for our example the prophet Samuel, who performed justice upon Agag with his own hand, saying, "as thy sword has made women childless, so shall thy mother be childless among women," a very proper punishment for tyrants, who advance themselves above the reach of all justice, except the prayers of the people, and the dagger of an Ehud. Providence and Nature have ever united devotion and a javelin in the hands of a Judith, and a Jael, to bring down an Holofernes, and a Sisera; because tyrants are such devils as cannot be cast out by prayer and fasting, unless aided by the workman's hammer. Those weapons unite Heaven and Earth to govern such men as will not be governed by civil laws, that every man might, agreeable to the Gospel, reap what he sows, and receive the same measure which he has meted out to others. We may complain with Jeremiah and say, "Why do the wicked prosper and the treacherous wax fat? How long shall the land mourn, and the herbs of the field wither?" We may add, that America resembles the state of the Jews upon the rivers of Babylon; for she has long hung her harps upon the willows, and forgot the mirth of Zion: "her children are gone forth, and are not; each one is crying, Woe is me, for I am hurt; my wound is grievous, and I must bear it; her pastors are brutish, their work is the work of errors, the land is in mourning; her spoilers are seated upon high places to keep peace from all flesh;" and no Moses, no Ehud, no Samuel, no Samson, no Jehoida, no Jael, nor Judith, hath appeared with a patriotic dagger, to do justice upon our tyrants, and save a sinking country! Surely this is not for want of patriots, but for the want of truly understanding the laws of God, nature, and civil society, which permit all men to kill thieves, breaking up houses in the night, lest they should escape justice by the help of darkness. Tyrants are worse robbers than the midnight thieves, for they hold themselves above justice, and the laws of civil society, which renders it necessary to repel force by force, and restore perfect liberty, the genuine fruit of law. If this is not the case, if laws of society bind us to submit to the usurpers acting opposite to law, a solitary life in the state of nature is preferable to civil society; but experience has taught the world, that there is no protection out of civil society, and in a state of nature we are all Ishmaels, whose hands are against one another. Men enter into civil societies, but not barely to exist, which they might do dispersed as other animals, but to live happy and agreeable to the dignity of human nature. To effect this noble view, men agree to submit their passions and appetites to the laws of reason and justice; and whenever lust, avarice, and ambition, are not, and cannot be regulated by the laws of the state, social liberty ceases, and natural liberty revives, wherein every man is a soldier, a Moses, a Samson, and may without incurring the guilt of murder, kill those uncircumcised Philistines with a javelin or any other weapon. By thus doing, men act upon the first law which is self-preservation, against thieves, tigers, and beasts of prey, a law which is above all political precepts and rules, and superior to every opinion of the mind. Since it is lawful to use any means in destroying tyrants, let us act gloriously in so doing, and free our country of the noxious Congress, under whose usurpations thousands have been murdered, and tens of thousands have been plundered. Having thus briefly touched upon the laws of God, of nature, and of nations, respecting the freedom and the rights of men, I shall,

1st. Enquire whether Congress are usurpers and tyrants, or a legal body of men.

2nd. Prove it the duty of all Protestants to do justice on them as Samson did on the Philistines.

3rd. Point out the benefit and necessity of so doing. As to the first head, we shall find that Congress may claim with great justice and little honor, the dignity of being both usurpers and tyrants. The civil law describes him to be an usurper who governs without any right; and the tyrant is he who governs contrary to the laws. My business is to show who have a right to govern, and what makes the power just. Fathers have a natural right to govern their wives and children, because they defend and support them; and in return the wives and children owe and pay subjection and obedience. Civil society is made up of several independent families by general consent, or by the command of God. Nature and revelation point out the necessity of having some to rule, and others to obey the rules and laws appointed by God, or the people, who alone have the power to alter natural liberty, and establish civil societies. The rulers are to be obeyed so far as they command according to the laws, and no farther; and the great body of the people are the judges to determine when the rulers govern by the laws, and when they do not; for the people are the legislators, and subjects of their laws, and not subjects of their magistrates. Notwithstanding this, a servant by the laws of God may say, I will not be free, and can bind myself to serve forever. Ex. xxi, 5. And the same power is vested in every society, as appears from the history of Saul and David.

It is very true, that God appointed Saul to be king over the people, to punish them for their ingratitude, which rendered Saul's power absolute, and passive obedience and non-resistance of divine authority; but Samuel anointed David king, who after Saul's death was confirmed by the elders of Israel at Hebron. 2 Samuel xi. 3. Those elders were the deputies of the people, authorized to limit David's kingly power; for before his inauguration, they obliged him by compact to govern justly, i. e. to protect the good, and to execute wrath upon the evil. Thus David became a minister of God to rule for the good of his people. Hence it is plain that all just power of government originates from God or the people; therefore, all who arrogate to themselves the power of governing, and cannot produce a commission from God or the people, are usurpers and tyrants, who may oppress but cannot govern. To such a power, people may be subject for wrath, but not for conscience sake.

After what has been suggested, have we not reason and a natural right to ask Congress, " who made you rulers over us? If God, why have not you published your commission? If the people, where was the place that we assembled? when did we give our consent? who were our elders to confirm your mighty power?"*

---

*True it is that near one hundred persons convened at Wethersfield, according to an advertisement signed by one Thomas Seymour, a lawyer, and chose a member to represent in Congress the County of Hartford, containing above sixty thousand souls. But it is presumed that previous to the choice of members of Congress, the question *whether there should be a Congress*, ought to have been put to the vote. That, however, was artfully evaded; a vast majority of the people were thereby divested of their weight in the Colony, as it would have been in the highest degree absurd and nugatory to have voted for members of a Congress *which did not exist*, and which they would not have suffered to exist, had a fair opportunity been given for their votes on that point. This

Whenever Congress shall answer these important and natural questions, and prove their authority to be from heaven or of men, I will gladly quit my chains, and submit to their dominion. Until these questions are duly answered, I will view my dungeon as my palace, and continue to say, if changing the government established by our ancestors, without our consent, or that of the king, or the nation of which we are a part; if dissolving charters, oaths, laws, and establishing iniquity by the bayonet; if taking away men's lives, liberty, and property, by Committees of Safety, the Inquisition, and Star Chamber Court in America; if maintaining rebellion by force and fraud to the benefit of a junto, and to the destruction of the people, of property; if these things denote what is tyranny, Congress cannot, with all its impudence, but own itself composed of the greatest tyrants that ever disgraced human nature. Congress having done all this, and commanded themselves to be prayed for as the supreme authority of America; they have left us in the state either of David to pray for deliverance from cruel and unreasonable men. or to pray like the woman of Syracuse for Dionysius.

I shall now add some outward marks given of ancient tyrants, to show the violence and deceit of Congress. "Tyrants" says Tacitus, "subvert laws and government under color of defending the rights and liberties of the people; and when they have got sufficient power, they rob the people of all their rights." Plato says, "Tyrants practice contrary to physicians, who purge us of our evil humors, but they, of our purest blood." Machiavel says, "Tyrants provide for ministers, when they flatter and torture Scripture, to prove usurpers lawful governors." Aristotle says, "The most successful art of tyrants, is to pretend great love for God and Religion." In these things we know Congress have excelled St. Oliver, and taught us that in godliness is great gain; and that preaching and praying lead to other kingdoms besides that of heaven; we are also taught that its arms are not carnal, but protestant; for they have overcome the church in defiance of all her prayers and tears. Had not modern Christians preferred the honor of being governed by a Protestant Congress. they might have had preaching for their tenths, instead of paying life, liberty, and property. To their comfort be it spoken, Congress manages the spiritual and temporal sword with as much dexterity as the Pope of Rome. Further evidence need not be produced of the tyranny of Congress, unless to such men as have great faith and little understanding; therefore since we both see and feel the merciless power of those beasts of prey, I shall proceed, secondly, to prove it the duty of all Protestants to do justice on Congress, as Samson did on the Philistines. Among us are two sects of Christians who daily pray to be delivered from the tyranny of those uncircumcised Philistines, but conscientiously differ about the mode; the one expects the Lord to remove them;

---

was the case throughout most of the Colonies. The Congress once formed in that unfair manner, decreed that members in future should be elected only by the true friends of America; that is, such as should abjure their king and sign the league and covenant; so that three-fourths of the Colony of Connecticut have never given a vote even for a *Member.*

the other expects that deliverance will be given by a Samson, armed with the jawbone of an ass. The Tories believe patience to be the only lawful cure, when under the power of usurpers and tyrants; the Whigs believe the safety of the people to be the first law, and laws to be above all rulers; and that kings and governors are accountable for their conduct at the bar of the community.

Here is the creed of those two sects touching lawful rulers; but I must remind them, without condemning either, that no people of sober sense ever gave up justice and liberty in duty and conscience, to usurpers and tyrants, who are Ishmaels, and wholly excluded all human protection, because they are enemies to societies, subverters of laws, and murderers of individuals; it is for this reason justice dispenses with her forms, and leaves tyrants and usurpers in the number of those savage beasts who herd not together, but defend themselves by their own strength, and prey upon all weaker animals. Would our Whigs and Tories reflect a few moments upon the nature of civil society, and upon what Tully says of laws, magistrates and people, they would discover laws to be above magistrates, as they are above individuals. It follows, that, when the depravity of men's wills renders them unfit to live in human society, it is murder in the community to let them live. If, then, in the land of peace, legal rulers degenerate into tyrants, weary people, and merit death, what deserve usurpers and tyrants, who, like the swellings of Jordan, sweep the world of safety by their iron rods?

Since we know that usurpers hold themselves above all justice but the stroke of some generous hand, we are to consider laws of civil society in regard to them as cobwebs, and no longer act like the Athenians, who punished only little thieves. If we were beasts, we should have a right to protect ourselves against our enemies; and as men and Christians, we cannot have less by entering into civil society. Let us, then, awake from slumber, and convince those men who shun justice in the court, that *they shall meet it in their beds;* for they are armed against all, and all may lawfully arm against them. Nothing is more absurd than to kill thieves, vipers, and bears, to prevent their cruel designs, and at the same time preserve Congress from acting much worse than the others intended. No one can any longer doubt of the lawfulness of destroying public robbers, whenever prudence points out the way, since the laws of God and men make it lawful to extirpate private robbers. Let us live in constant faith that Heaven will soon sanctify some patriotic hand, armed with *some sacred weapon*, to bring down that bloody and deceitful house, which holds its existence not only to the misery, but to the everlasting infamy of Protestant America. The action is not only *lawful,* but *glorious* in idea, and *immortal* in its reward! Were not these sentiments supported by the wise and grave among the ancients, and the Jesuits and Protestants of the last century, I should not have preached them in this dreary abode. But to wipe all doubts from your minds, I will produce some authorities to support what has been said.

Tertullian says, "Against common enemies and traitors to the rights and majesty of the people everything is lawful."

Xenophon says, "The Grecians erected in their temples among their gods, statues for those that killed tyrants."

It was enacted by the Valerian law, that "whoever made themselves rulers without command from the people, were tyrants, and might be killed."

Plutarch says, "It is lawful to kill usurpers without trial."

Polybius says, "Men of the greatest virtues conspired against and killed tyrants."

Cicero applauds Brutus for conspiring against Julius Cæsar, "What action, O! Jupiter, more glorious, more worthy of eternal memory?"

At Athens, according to Solon's law, "death was decreed for tyrants and their abettors."

Plato says, "When tyrants cannot be expelled by law, the citizens may use secret practices." The reason is, community must be preserved from the rage of tyrants, who can receive no injustice, either by force or fraud. Thus you have the opinions of the ancients; while the history of Rome, Christian and Germanic States and England teaches us the same doctrines and practices.

The Jesuits, in Spain and France, have ever held the knife of justice as a law for tyrants. Our fathers in the last century erected a high court of justice for a tyrant, his reverend and right reverend abettors. Congress and the governors of our respective States, have sufficiently proved by their practices, that the killing of tyrants and their adherents is not murderous, but truly Christian, upon which priciple, America armed against her rightful king; and, for the same reason, we that love our country *may destroy the self-created Congress*, which sits in Cæsar's chair, above citation, or a court of justice. What Whig or Tory will be content with formal remedies which are far off?—what justice can we expect from malefactors who have the power to hang and assassinate their rightful judges? Consonant to what been said about tyrants and usurpers, stands the law of God, viz: "*He that acts presumptuously shall surely die.*" In such a case, every man is judge and executioner. By this law, Moses slew the Egyptians; Ehud slew Eglon; Samson, the Philistines; Samuel, Agag; and Jehoida, Athaliah. By parity of reason, every Cicero and Brutus may smite hip and thigh, the Congress, its Mattans and Janizaries, for they have presumptuously smote our children and countrymen with whips of brass, fed them with passive obedience, and clothed them in prisons with famine, nakedness and death. It cannot be infamous to destroy them by whom all America is oppressed; because Moses is immortalized in the records of God, for killing an individual who oppressed another. This we may depend on, that whatever was lawful and right in Moses, Ehud, and Samson, is lawful and right for Whigs and Tories in America; for the laws of retaliation and justice, are the same here as they were in Jewry.

Some people object, and say that these examples taken from Holy Scripture, were of men sent by God to kill those several tyrants, and have we not the like commission. Milton, of immortal fame, has answered this objection. Says he, "If God commanded tyrants to be killed, it is a sign that tyrants ought to die." Besides, we read that all the people of the land rejoiced, and the city had rest after Athaliah was slain with the sword; that the people obeyed Jehoinda as king for the good he had done, and buried him among their princes; which was but half the reward given to this patriot, for the divine historian has recorded his generous deed in the book of God, where the last man that lives shall read his eulogies, and the just command which he gave, to kill the followers of Athaliah; a proper warning to our Protestant Levites, our generals and committees of safety, to repent, lest they likewise perish with their masters, by the workman's hammer. But the objection supposes what in fact is not true; for Samson and those other worthies who killed tyrants, never alleged the command of God for what they did, but defended themselves on the plea of retaliation—"As they did unto me, so have I done unto them." God had not appeared to Moses in the bush prior to his smiting the Egyptian; and Jehoinda had only the call which is common to all men—to do natural justice when legal cannot be had. Some people pretend to believe Congress are not usurpers and tyrants, because traffic and appeals are carried on under their dominion, which argues a tacit consent of the public.

To prove these men mistaken, I need only say, that commerce and pleading were carried on in Rome under Caligula and Nero, yet those who conspired against them were not deemed rebels, but were eternized for their virtue.

Having pointed out the marks and practices of tyrants and usurpers, and shown the lawfulness and glory of killing them, I shall now, in the third and last place, hint the benefits and necessity of doing it.

What is our present condition? Are we not slaves and living instruments of Congress, Washington, and the Protestant Ministers, and their Romish allies? Poor wretches, indeed, are we! Cozened out of peace, religion, liberty, and property; robbed of the blessings of Judah; and cursed with the spirit and burden of Issachar, by a set of men without virtue, or the generous vices attending greatness? It is no wonder that slaves should lose their courage with their virtue, for who can fight for Cæsar* that despises them, or for Nero, when every victory gained for him confirms their bondage, and adds a new rivet to their chains. Thus we are compelled to live, or not to live at all; deliverance is not to be hoped for from our patience, because usurpers are never modest but in the hour of weakness: nor was any government ever managed with justice, that was gained by villainy. Liberty and bondage are now before us; those who

---

* The American Loyalists have little reason to confide in the mercy of the British army and navy, who have uniformly for seven years treated them much worse than they have the Rebels; and should they judge the English nation by the severity of its military forces, which have killed and plundered more Loyalists than Rebels, no nation could censure them if they, like Congress, should buy their good will, at the expense of their allegiance.

choose liberty, are to kill the uncircumcised Congress. Yet I find some men scruple to kill their oppressors with a dagger in the dark, although they allow it lawful to destroy a thief that comes unarmed to rob; those men seem to forget the law of self-preservation, the danger of open force, and that tyrants are such devils as rend the body in the act of exorcism.

How can it be lawful to kill oppressors in an open field, prepared to rob the men they mean to murder, and unlawful to kill such villains in the dark, without hazard to the patriot or to the commonwealth? If it is expedient to lance an imposthume to save a life, it is lawful to lance the Congress to save the liberties of our country; for those boars of the wilderness have broken down the walls of the vineyard, and destroyed the vintage with unlimited power, which always subverts civil society, and turns a Cicero into a Caligula. Our religion, and all we call valuable, are in danger. Despotism is now predominant; and America, once the asylum of Protestants persecuted beyond the seas, is sold to the mother of harlots, and will soon be cursed with the Inquisition to establish Congress and its generals, as the hereditary lords of the land. Tyranny and oppressions have increased with the age of Congress, and our deliverance depends upon the virtuous spears of an injured people, or upon the generosity of our tyrants by hanging themselves. But since we know they lack this virtue, nothing remains for the patriots but to do justice upon well-erected gibbets. Whatever Congress may think of this proposed exaltation, they may depend upon it, that eight-tenths of the people would rejoice at the sight, and the children yet unborn would be happy under their rightful king.

Some serious Whigs who have lost their courage with their fortunes, groan under their present burdens and say, "we fear the consequence of destroying "Congress." I answer, could we be in a worse condition by a change, the bare desire of a change would be a sign of madness. Common sense forbids me to undergo certain misery, for fear of contingent evils; or to let a fever rage because there is danger of taking physic. I am now in prison, where I must infallibly perish if I am not relieved; and shall I refuse deliverance from this darksome dungeon for fear of being confined in some other place? Heaven forbid such madness! Let us remember the rock from whence we were hewn. Had we not ancestors in the last century who preferred liberty and religion in this howling wilderness, to despotism and persecution in Britannia's fertile fields? Are we so far degenerated as to bow down to tyrants and usurpers? Our fathers resisted lions, and killed tyrants without committing murder and shall we submit to wolves and beasts of prey to let usurpers live? No! let the examples of Ehud, Samson, Moses, and Cromwell, lead us back to glory, virtue, and religion. If America can produce no such heroes, we must exclaim with the children of Israel, "Would to God we had died in the land of Egypt, where we sat by the fleshpots, and did eat bread to the full;" for then, as Cicero says, "the quality of our master would have graced our condition as slaves." We have rights of civil society to restore; we have honor, virtue, and religion to maintain; let us therefore take the first prudent opportunity to revenge our wrongs, and kill those tyrants who are lurking in every corner to spy out our motions, and murder the innocent. Their motto is to destroy or be destroyed. Therefore, let safety rouse us into action, let Fame reward the sacred hand of him that gives the fatal blow; let his name live forever with Cato, and with Brutus. O, how I long to save my country by one heroic immortal action! but alas! my chains and dreary mansion, where the light of conscience reigns without the light of the sun, of the moon, or the stars!* To you, my virtuous countrymen, who are free of the chains with which I am loaded, I conclude my address. It is now in your power to circumcise, to put down those uncircumcised tyrants, and to restore yourselves to your social rights. You know the action that will do the business, and which shall register your names among the Gods and bravest men. Patriotism warms your souls, and thousands are burning with ambition to join and save your country from Romish bondage. Make haste! for the spirit of understanding causeth me to speak in the language of Zophar, "Let death and destruction fall upon" Congress "because they have oppressed and forgotten the poor; let a fire not blown, consume them; if they escape the iron weapons, strike them through with a bow of steel, for knowest thou not this of old, since man was placed upon earth, that the triumphing of the wicked is short, and the joy of the hypocrite but for a moment."

And although the devils are come down in great wrath, with power in their mouths, and in their tails; although their heads reach the clouds, and though they do hurt with their tails; yet their murders, their fornication, and their thefts shall be revealed, and the earth shall rise against them, "to feed them with the poison of asps. The vipers tongue shall pierce them through, and their greatness shall be chased away as a vision of the night. "This is the portion of the wicked."

Finis.

N. B. The notes on pp. 46, 50, and 52, are by the author of the sermon.

THE GOSPEL FURNISHED BY THE STATE.

A few years after the establishment of the prison by legislative act, provision was made for religious services one-half of each Sunday by uniting with the society at East Granby, in paying a stipulated salary to the clergyman officiating. For many years the services were held in the nail-shop, the most refractory of the prisoners being chained to their nail blocks. The seats of the general audience were upon the level ground (without floor) while the elevated platform used by the guards, was improvised as a pulpit, and the choir was

---

* Vide the History of Connecticut, page 175 published by J. Bew, Pater Noster Row; where is a just description of the infernal prison at Symsbury, 40 yards below the surface of the earth.

composed of any neighbors who felt disposed to volunteer for the occasion.

It can reasonably be supposed that the nail-shop preaching was a wonderful contrast to the preceeding discourse of the Rev. Licentiate Baxter; but Baxter's Tory audience in the dungeon considered his preaching sound and reliable, no doubt,—notwithstanding any slight discrepancies in text or argument.

A comfortable chapel was subsequently built, where, each Sunday, the guards with their long muskets, the citizens and the prisoners all assembled in the same room. No Sunday-school nor library for the prisoners' use ever enlightened the dismal precincts of old Newgate; those blessings were reserved for the new prison at Wethersfield.

In 1781 Congress applied to Gov. Trumbull of Connecticut (known by the appellation of "Brother Jonathan"), for the use of the mines as a prison "for the reception of British prisoners of war, and for the purpose of retaliation." The Governor laid the matter before the Assembly, who agreed to the proposition, and requested him to furnish Congress with the estimates, but as a termination of the war was anticipated soon, the negotiation ended.

This place won a reputation for strength and security throughout the country, though there was more strength in its name than in reality. Six years previously, Gen. Washington sent several prisoners to be confined in the dungeon, whom he regarded as "atrocious villains." The following letter from him will be read with interest. It is directed to the Committee of Safety at Simsbury:

CAMBRIDGE, Dec. 7th, 1775.

Gentlemen:—The prisoners which will be delivered you with this, having been tried by a court martial and deemed to be such flagrant and atrocious villains, that they cannot by any means be set at large, or confined in any place near this camp, were sentenced to Simsbury, in Connecticut. You will therefore be pleased to have them secured in your jail, or in such other manner as to you shall seem necessary, so that they cannot possibly make their escape. The charges of their imprisonment will be at the Continental expense.

I am, &c.,

GEORGE WASHINGTON.

The vindictive cruelty of the Tories is shown in Barber's Historical Collections of Connecticut. The narrative is substantially thus:

On the night following the 14th of March, 1780, the house of Capt. Ebenezer Dayton then residing in the town of Bethany, was broken into and robbed by seven men, who were Tories, and headed by a British officer, Alex. Graham* from Long Island. Mr. Dayton's house was situated nearly opposite where the first meeting-house in Bethany was erected, about half a mile south of the present Congregational church, and about ten miles northwest of New Haven. The particulars of this robbery were obtained from the Rev. Mr. Dayton, son of Capt. Dayton mentioned above. Mr. Dayton, who belonged to Long Island, was, on account of his attachment to the American cause, obliged to leave that island, and bring his effects with him to Bethany. A number of men, some of his neighbors, were obliged to leave the island for the same cause, and brought a considerable quantity of money with them, and for a while resided in Mr. Dayton's house. With these facts the robbers appear to have become acquainted. At the time of the robbery, Mr. Dayton was absent on business at Boston, and the men who had been staying in the house had left the day before, so that there was no one in the house but his wife, Mrs. Phœbe Dayton, three small children, and two colored servant children.

About midnight, while they were all asleep, the window in the bedroom where Mrs. Dayton was sleeping, was burst in at once; seven armed men rushed in, passed through the room, and immediately rushed into the chambers, expecting (it is supposed) to find the men who had left the day before. While they were upstairs, Mrs. Dayton went to the front part of the house, raised the window, and endeavored to alarm the neighbors. Mr. Hawley, the minister of the parish,

---

* Graham, it was afterwards ascertained, was a deserter, from the American army and also held a commission from the British general, Howe, to recruit Tories for the British army. On searching him the commission was found in his pocket, to which also he made confession.

and Dr. Hooker, the physician of the place, both lived within twenty rods distance, both had lights in their houses at the time, and both heard the alarm, but did not know from whence it proceeded. The robbers, hearing Mrs. Dayton, came down, and tearing a sheet into strips, tied her hands behind her, made her sit in a chair, and placed her infant (about six months old) in her lap, while one of the robbers, placing the muzzle of his gun near her head, kept her in this position for about two hours, while the house was thoroughly ransacked from top to bottom. As Mr. Dayton had been a merchant and peddler, a large quantity of goods were found and the most valuable packed in sacks and bundles. Most of the articles were of foreign production,— worsted goods, coats, cloaks, ladies' gowns, silk and linen handkerchiefs, various kinds of linen goods, silver shoe-buckles, a spy-glass, two muskets and their accoutrements, four halberds, (a pike with hatchet near the point), etc., besides four hundred and fifty pounds in gold, silver, and copper coin, and two hundred Continental paper-dollars.

To appease their hunger, they ordered the servants to place upon the table in the kitchen the best which the kitchen and pantry afforded; which orders were obeyed in silence under close surveillance of the robbers.

Some of them secured a light and went into the cellar, where they found abundance of liquors which they let out upon the ground after supplying their own needs. What they could not conveniently carry off they wantonly destroyed, breaking in pieces all the crockery, furniture, etc. The whole amount of property carried off and destroyed, including bonds, notes, etc., amounted to five thousand pounds. The robbers left the house about two o'clock, and went to a place in Middlebury, called Gunn-Town, where they were secreted in a cellar by a family who were friendly to the British cause. While they were on their way to Gunn-Town, they met a young man by the name of Chauncey Judd,* of

---

* The biographer of Chauncey Judd, in describing the sufferings he

Waterbury, on a bridge, who had been to see a young lady he afterwards married. Fearing he might discover them they took him along with them. In the cellar kitchen where they were all secreted there was a well. Into this well they talked of putting young Chauncey; but the old lady of the house begged they would not think of it, as it would *spoil the water!* They stayed in the house a number of days: afterwards they went to Oxford, where they were secreted for several days longer in a barn; from thence they went to Stratford, took a whale-boat, and crossed over to Long Island. The people at Derby, having received information of their passing through that place, two whale-boats and crews, commanded by Capt. William Clarke and Capt James Harvey, pursued them to the Island, and were fortunate enough to catch all of them but one, just within the British lines, and recover their booty. They were brought back, tried, and condemned. Graham the ringleader was executed and the others were sent to Newgate; they, however, broke prison, and some of them fled to Nova Scotia.

Among the robbers who plundered Mr. Dayton's house, was a Tory by the name of Henry Wooster, who was sentenced by the Superior Court of New Haven county, to pay a fine of fifty pounds, and to be imprisoned four years in Newgate. From an interesting account written of him by an acquaintance of the family, it appears that after his confinement in prison, he made a key which would unlock his fetters in the cavern, being careful, of course, to replace them before

---

endured while in the hands of the banditti says: "He had endured hardships which were enough to crush one much stronger than he. Indeed he was for several days partially insane. The shock to his nervous system from the repeated imminent prospect of death increased by his severe bodily sufferings had completely broken him down. Often would he awake from a sort of stupor and cry "Hurrah for King George!" (having been compelled to say so by his captors). During their flight down the river and across the Sound he had been wholly unprotected from the wind, and had almost perished from the cold, his hands had been frost bitten, and some of his fingers remained crippled for life. He never recovered from the effects of his hardships, but continued in delicate health until his death.

going up to his work each morning. The writer says:

"One of the first things he attempted was to make thorough exposition of the caverns, to see if there was any possible way of escape. For this purpose he forced himself into one of the drains which discharged the waters of the mine. This, after the use of the mines as a prison, had been carefully built up with stone and mortar, leaving only a narrow channel which was supposed to be thoroughly secured by iron bars. Watching opportunities, he contrived to conceal in his clothes, fragments of nail-rods, and carry them below. With these he picked out little by little, bits of mortar, until the bars were loosened so as to permit their removal; in the same way he enlarged the drain in some of its narrowest places, and after many weeks of hard toil, found himself near the outer orifice. Redoubled exertions followed, in which he was aided as far as possible by other convicts who had the use of their hands. It was a hard and dangerous task. At one time while far within, he gave himself up for lost. A stone overhead which he had partially loosened fell into the drain behind him, effectually closing the passage and debarring his return. Unable to turn round or reach the stone with his hands, he concluded that his last hour was come, and that he must perish in his terrible prison! His cries for help could scarcely be heard by the other convicts, and if heard, it was doubtful whether they could relieve him. With great effort, however, he found he could push the stone a little with his foot. But would it pass the whole distance? for if there was one single place in the passage too small, he would be inextricably shut in. By bracing himself against the sides and pressing with all his strength, he succeeded at length in pushing the stone to a hollow spot, which would permit him to pass over it. With desperate energy he crowded himself by, and at last emerged into the cavern just before the daybreak bell sounded to call the prisoners to their labor. He had been in the drain all night, and came forth bleeding and nearly exhausted. He was obliged to conceal his suffering condition from the guard, otherwise it would lead to a search and exposure; so replacing with the help of his comrades his irons and clothing, (for he had gone into the drain naked) he dragged himself up the ladder to his work. If his bruised and haggard condition was noticed at all by the officers, it excited no remark, the evidences of fighting and sleeplessness being too common among the prisoners to awaken any suspicion.

"A few nights afterwards, having somewhat recovered from his bruises and sufferings, it was deemed practicable to escape, and Wooster with several others who were able to unfasten their fetters succeeded in crawling through the passage and fled to the woods an hour before day. Their escape was soon discovered and the alarm given. Nearly all were re-taken and brought back to prison. Wooster more tricky, hid himself in the top of a dark hemlock upon the mountain until the next night, when he began his flight, and finally succeeded in reaching the coast near New London, and made his way on board an English vessel, where he enlisted in the British service. * * * * * * Four years after the termination of the war, one day in the dusk of the evening, a traveller came to the house of Henry Wooster, Sen., in Derby, and asked permission to lodge there that night. He was weary and footsore, he said, and could go no further. Hospitality in such cases was a habit of New England, and his request was granted. Mrs. Wooster was then engaged in preparing a kettle of hasty-pudding for the family supper, and at her invitation the traveller partook of the repast. In the course of it, he contrived to turn the conversation upon her own family, and especially of her absent son. She recounted with a mother's partiality his amiable qualities, his manly strength and agility. Won by the interest he seemed to manifest in her story, she bewailed the sad occasion of his falling in with a stranger who had persuaded him to go off on a foolish expedition as she said, against a *piratical Yankee*, and that in consequence, he got into Newgate prison, but after a while he with others broke out, since which she had heard nothing from him and presumed he must be dead.

"At length, after hearing the sad story of the good woman the traveller assumed his natural speech and manner and announced himself as her missing son! At first she was incredulous, and unable to recognize him, till opening the bosom of his shirt he showed her a mark on his breast. This well-remembered mark convinced her of his identity. She fell on his neck and like the father of the prodigal, wept tears of joy over her long-lost boy."

Old Newgate Prison.

"With flickering candle down the dread descent,
To darkest depths I slowly make my way;
The aged ladder creaks from many a rent,
And spirit-voices of a former day
In murmuring whispers warn of dangers there;
Of unseen Furies who with silent tread
Will lead me on to labyrinthal snare
Where none escape, but number with the dead."

Newgate was at this time used by the State for the confinement of criminals, and they were kept chiefly at work in making wrought nails. It was not until 1790 that it was established permanently as a State prison. It is said to have been the design to employ the convicts in working the mines, which for a while was practiced, but it was soon found that they must necessarily have for that work, precisely the right kind of tools for digging out, and they several times used them for that purpose. This reason, with the consequent necessity of keeping so strong a guard, both day and night, finally induced them to abandon the employment. In 1790 an act was passed constituting Newgate a permanent prison, and providing for the erection of the necessary buildings.

The expense was limited by legislative act to seven hundred and fifty pounds. The overseers were authorized to make the works very secure; to appoint a keeper and a guard not exceeding ten persons—which number was afterwards increased to seventeen. After this a better system of management was pursued until the convicts were removed to the new prison at Wethersfield.

A wooden palisade, mounted with iron spikes, was constructed, inclosing half an acre of ground, within which, workshops and other buildings were placed, and a deep trench was opened on the western side. The wooden enclosure remained until 1802, when a strong stone-wall twelve feet high, was laid in its place, which is now standing. A brick building was erected in the centre of the yard for the officers and privates, in the rear and lower part of which a stone apartment was afterwards constructed directly over the mouth of the cavern, and in this room the most quiet prisoners were occasionally kept. This was denominated the "stone jug."

About the year 1815, a building nearly fifty feet long, was erected on the southeast corner of the yard. The lower story was occasionally used for cells, and the upper one for a chapel, where services were usually held once a day on Sundays. Another building adjoining next west, the lower story of which was used as a cooper shop, hospital, and kitchen, and the upper as a shoemaker's shop. In the northeast corner of the yard, another building was used as a wagon-shop. Eight or nine years later a large building of stone and brick was put up on the west side of the yard, and a tread-mill, for grinding grain, was constructed in it, principally by labor of the convicts. Cells were provided in this building for female prisoners, and rooms for officers, &c.

The passage down the shaft into the caverns, is upon a ladder fastened upon one side, and resting on the bottom. At the foot of this passage commences a gradual descent for a considerable distance, all around being solid massive rock or ore. The passages extend many rods in different directtions, some of them even leading under the cellars of the dwellings in the neighborhood. In two of the passages are deep wells of water, one of which is eighty feet from the surface; they served for a free circulation of air to the inmates of this gloomy place, and were sometimes used for shafts through which to lift the ore, when the business was carried on. On the sides and niches of the cavern, cabins were built of heavy planks, within which straw was placed for their beds. The prisoners were locked in them each night, but frequently in their carousals, they would break or unfasten the locks and tear their cabins to pieces. The horrid gloom of this dungeon can be realized only by those who pass among its solitary windings. The impenetrable vastness supporting the awful mass above, impending as if ready to crush one to atoms: the dripping water trickling like tears from its sides; the unearthly echoes responding to the voice, all conspire to strike the beholder aghast with amazement and horror. These caverns and their precincts, from their antiquity, and the dramas which have been performed in and around them, will long be considered a classic place.

The caverns have generally been extremely favorable to the health and longevity of the occupants, which is attributed to some medical quality in the mineral rock. It is a curious fact, that many of the convicts having previously taken the itch, or other loathsome diseases, while confined in the county jails, which were very filthy, on being for a few weeks kept in the caverns at night, entirely uncovered; and it is perhaps still more strange, that those who came apparently in health, generally had for a short time cutaneous eruptions, which appeared to work out of their blood.

A writer upon the subject observes:

"From the various windings and other causes, it is not cold there, even in the severest weather; and strange as it may seem, it has been satisfactorily ascertained, that the mercury ranged eight degrees lower in the lodging apartments of the prisoners in the warmest days of summer, than it does in the coldest in the winter. This phenomenon is attributed to the circumstance of the cavities in the rocks being stopped with snow, ice, and frost in the winter, which prevents so free a circulation of air as is enjoyed in the summer. On the 18th of January 1811, at eight o'clock A. M., the mercury stood in the cavern at fifty-two degrees; and in the open air, as soon after as it was practicable for a person to get up from the cavern (which could not have exceeded five minutes), it fell to one degree below 0."

A newspaper correspondent relates his adventures in the caverns as follows:—

"The wall with its brick bastion and guardhouse, 6x6, and 12 feet high, the latter seated like a marten-box on the former, peeped through the trees suddenly. It has stood almost three-quarters of a century. On the stone above the gate that looks east at the black curtain of the mountain, are engraved the syllables, "Newgate, 1801."

The sentry-box and bastion I have described project so as to command the grated windows in the south wall. The enclosure is square and contains about two acres. It stands square with the sun. On the west the mountain is terraced up to the prison, yielding three precipices of 25 feet in height, and rendering escape possible only by three desperate break-neck leaps after scaling the main wall. On the west a deep moat doubles the danger. To the south wall clings the long stone building occupied by the guards and the workshops, whose guns commanded the whole length of masonry on the east. The wooden roof and the floors are warped and shrunken, but the iron rings and staples in the wall have rusted very little since desperate men set them clanking with every stir of their ankles.

Sam and I stood for half a minute peering down into the dark, and said nothing. Sam tested the wooden ladder with his hand.

"I'll try it first, I'm the lighter," said I, dropping down out of sight with a leap. "Stay here till I call."

After descending about fifty feet I found myself at the bottom of the shaft with Sam's face peering in at the top like a portrait set in a square frame.

"Solid ground," I shouted up the ladder. The light was shut out suddenly, and Sam began the descent. Lighting the candles and leaving one of them in a crevice at the foot of the shaft, at Sam's instance, I took the other and led the way down a series of stone steps, thirty or forty in number, dipping away to the east under the mountain. The roof was very low, and the candle gave so little light, that I was compelled to feel my way forward with my walking-stick. Here, after following several galleries till they ended in solid rock, I finally struck the right one, and groped forward twenty or thirty feet into the caverns —an irregular series of galleries, where the prisoners used to sleep, and where old Prince the negro who had once been servant to an officer under Gen. Washington, died shackled to the wall, and rotted where he died. The old man was too decrepit to work, and was hence not looked after by the prison officials.* A considerable excavation has taken place at this point, resulting in a central cavern bristling with nooks in the rock of somewhat irregular depth. These were used as sleeping-places by the prisoners, and still exhibited the remains of bunks.

Striking a gallery leading northeast, and still dipping under the mountain, I followed on, candle in hand, bumping my head against the roof, now and then, and feeling my way step by step with my walking-stick. The water dropped from the roof; the floor tipped on the east until the water was more than ankle-deep; the candle burned dimly and spluttered. A single drop of water might at any moment have extinguished it.

By and by, gleamed in the distance something like water with the light falling upon it from above, and Sam and I staggered on, expecting at every step to get a ducking, and liable to it with the merest unlucky slip of the foot. A slimy ooze covered the floor on the west side of the gallery, and our feet squashed at every step and clung to the mud like plasters. After crawling about thirty feet in this way, our progress was barred by a sheet of water about twenty feet in breadth. Sounding it with my walking-stick, and finding it too deep to be

---

* Prince never was shackled. but was a harmless old negro, and during all the last years of his life enjoyed the freedom of the prison.

waded, I took my bearings and retraced my steps, with a view to find the hundred-foot shaft, famous in traditions of the prison as the spot where the tory in revolutionary days, tried to escape by climbing out on a rope, and fell nearly a hundred feet from the top to the bottom. He had spent his last $50 in bribing a neighbor to unfasten the trap—there was no wall in those days—with what avail they tell you as an evidence that God strongly disapproved of tories.

Once more in the main cavern, after testing several galleries of from ten to thirty feet in length, I finally worked east and down until my walking-stick, with which I felt my way like a blind man with his staff, encountered no floor, and the faintest possible glimmer of light filtered in from above. Here was a perpendicular jump of ten feet, and a bar upon which the prisoners were in the habit of swinging themselves down into the gallery leading away to the southeast.

This shaft is round, and terminates at the top just within the gate by the east wall, twenty feet from the workshop. It is a trifle over a hundred feet deep, I should say, and was formerly furnished with a rope and windlass for lifting out the ore. The rope still dangles loosely from the top, but the remaining appurtenances have been removed.

As it was impracticable to drop into the gallery at this point, Sam suggested that the exploration should be abandoned; but, having retraced twenty feet or more. I detected a gallery pushing to the southeast at an acute angle, and turned into it, Sam consenting to wait at the corner till I came back. This tunnel strikes the one out of which the main shaft opens about twenty feet to the south, by a gradual but exceedingly rapid and risky descent. So I found myself at last at the deepest point in the mine, in the tunnel terminating in that fatal drain, where still lie the bones of prisoners who tried to escape by that desperate route, and died at dead of night away under the mountain, self-buried, but coffined in solid rock.*

I followed this tunnel, which was a trifle higher in the roof than the rest, till the water was too deep to admit of penetrating further. Water dripped from the roof, from the walls. As I turned a drop struck the wick of the candle, and it spluttered and went out, leaving me in a perfect darkness such as a man never experiences above ground. A little nervous I groped back, feeling for the first gallery to the left with my walking-stick, and stricken with a sudden fear, that I might have passed others unconsciously on my route, and might turn into the wrong one on my way back. It did not occur to me to shout to Sam, who was waiting for me not twenty rods off, till a sharp "come on!" away to the southwest enabled me to take my bearings and calculate my distances.

"Yes, directly; but my candle's out," I shouted, groping forward for ten or fifteen minutes, till my walking-stick indicated a break in the wall at the left. Here I shouted again, and was answered almost at my ear, Sam having felt his way down the gallery almost to its junction with the tunnel.

It was impossible to sit down, so our council of war had to be held standing. There were still difficulties to be encountered, and not the least one of them was imaginary. The candle at the foot of the ladder could not last many minutes longer, for an hour at least must have elapsed since our descent. To the left, then to the right, then to the left again, in the general direction of the gallery into which I had just turned, was agreed upon in council as the nearest

---

* Another fable, having a very slight foundation in the fact that several convicts *did* escape by that route;—but they all took their own bones with them.

way out, but in a route encumbered with abandoned galleries, there was no knowing how many might have to be tried before hitting the right one. However, it was useless to dawdle over that question, when the candle at the foot of the ladder might be going out.

So, taking the front, I laid my walking-stick horizontally against the wall, faced myself by it at right angles so as to look straight ahead, and groped along, muttering to myself that this must have been a rare place for a state prison, and conjuring up German stories of cobolds; or if, as the mining ballad runs,

> "The ghosts of mining men
> Revisit earth again,
> And make old mines their den,"

imagining spectral miners, and converting the trickle of water from the roof into the click of invisible implements.

A thud of my shoulder against something hard shook me out of my reverie or my reverie out of me, and putting out my hand I found it to be a wooden prop supporting the roof. I had noticed three or four of them in the main cavern—or congeries of galleries terminating in a central space—and this reassured me. Asking Sam to keep exactly in my tracks by putting his hands on my shoulders, I started due north as near as I could, waving my walking-stick to and fro in front of me, so as to develop any obstacle in the way before I bumped against it; for it was now impracticable to follow by the wall without doubling at least half a dozen abandoned galleries varying in length from ten to thirty feet, while, by stumbling directly across the central cavern the entrance to the gallery leading westward and upward to the foot of the ladder would be intercepted, and if the candle had gone out, it was possible that light enough might sift down through the fifty-foot shaft, though enclosed at the top, to furnish a clue to its position. So Sam and I stumbled on, hoping to get out in a few minutes, but a little nervous and shaky in our voices with the possibility of having to stay under ground. And I, for one, was growing a little drowsy for want of oxygen, and a trifle hungry besides.

I had nearly passed the entrance to the upward dipping tunnel, when Sam called attention to a kind of cloud of light at its end. The candle was out; but now the route was direct, and if the kind of cloud indicated the bottom of the shaft, there was an end to all apprehension. I turned and blundered up an inclined plane till my foot struck a stone step, succeeded by another, as I ascertained with my walking stick. It grew momentarily a little lighter, and fancies of cobold and miner's ghost flitted from my brain as stealthily as they had come. It would be poetic perhaps, to say that they folded their tent like the Arabs in Mr. Longfellow's ballad, and silently stole away, were it not that ghosts and cobolds are not reputed to live in tents, though very nomadic in their habits.

"So this was the Connecticut state prison from 1774 to 1827," quoth I, as I scrambled up the ladder after Sam had disappeared above ground.

Among the accidents which have occured to visitors, was that of Mrs. Christia Griswold of Poquonock, who while standing at the mouth of the shaft leading down into the cavern, accidentally stepped off, and fell the whole depth, striking on the rocky bottom. The buoyancy of her clothes, or some other cause, saved her life, though she received injuries from which she never recovered. A prisoner afterwards fell at the same place, fetters and all, without appearing to injure him, it is said, in the least.

A few years since a party of students were on a visit to the mines, when one of their number stepped into the shaft, and fell to the bottom, receiving injuries which caused his death in a few months. The descent upon the ladder is now accomplished by any one, and the trouble is well repaid by the interesting relics below. When Newgate was in full blast, it was a very popular place of resort for travellers and pleasure parties, as from a report of the overseers in 1810, it appears that about 5,400 persons visited the place annually.

The original manuscript of that report is now in possession of the author, written by Judge Samuel Woodruff, in 1810, he at that time being one of the overseers; and the following are extracts from some of his replies to certain questions propounded by a legislative committee:

"*Ans. to question 2nd.*—Health generally good when committed. A few afflicted with chronic complaints and perhaps one in nine or ten sorely afflicted with the veneral disease. One-third or more of the latter class have been cured. * * * With respect to cleanliness; when committed, the greater part come dirty, and at least one-fifth part covered with vermin. Much pains is taken to clean them of the vermin which could and would be effected were it not for the frequent recruits from the county prisons.

Ans. to question 3rd.—The price of a ration is 9cts. 5m. The component parts of a ration, 1lb. of beef or 3-4lb. of pork at 4cts 5m.; 1lb. of bread or flour, at 3cts.; 3 gills of peas or beans, or 2lbs. of potatoes, and 3 pints of *cider* at 2cts. In the summer the prisoners are supplied occasionally with greens, collected by the guard without expense to the State. The prisoners for two or three years past were fed with soup as often as one day in four, but on account of their universal dislike to it, they have been fed on soup for the last year, but one day in seven. This soup is composed of a ration made of 3-4lb. of beef 2 lbs. potatoes with a suitable quantity of Indian meal to thicken it.

Ans. to question 4th.—The winter clothing for prisoners consists of 2 check flannel shirts, a short coat, 1 pair pants of homemade cloth, 2 pairs of woolen stockings and one pair shoes. Their summer clothing consists of a change of tow-cloth frocks and trousers, with stockings and shoes. Their shirts, summer frocks, trousers, and stockings, are shifted and washed once a week, and are boiled in strong lye made of ashes which effectually destroys the vermin.

Ans. to question 5th.—The prisoners are lodged in huts or cabins made in the cavern. They are built on a floor elevated three feet above the ground, and are ranged on each side of a space which lies between them. The roofs and outer sides of these cabins are made close and tight with boards. The berths in these cabins are plentifully supplied with blankets, and generally with straw when the prisoners wish it. The straw is shifted as often as is necessary.

Ans. to question 6th.—The prisoners are secured by iron fetters round their ankles. While at work a chain fastened to a block is locked into these fetters, or round the ankle. For the more daring and refractory, heavier chains are occasionally used.

Ans. to question 9th.—No allowance is made to those prisoners who do more than their daily task. Formerly an allowance, of one penny on each pound of nails over the daily task, was allowed. But this practice for several years past has been discontinued; it was found this allowance induced them to slight their work, and to steal nails from each other at the forges."

It further appears by the above report, that the number of prisoners at that time was forty-six. The description of the rations as given would not indicate a very high state of culinary art; but however unsavory the qualities of that "soup," the *cider* was probably deemed a sufficient compensation for both that and the *vermin*.

By some, this place has been compared to the ancient Bastile of France, but the comparison is far from being correct, except in the frightful emotions which this dungeon is calculated to inspire. The floors and the roof of the Bastile were made of iron plates riveted upon iron bars. The walls were of stone and iron several feet in thickness; the whole being surrounded by walls, and a ditch twenty-five feet deep. The entrance to each cell was through three consecutive doors, secured by double locks. The scanty food, and the silent, unavailing grief, endured by the wretched victims of that dreadful abode, often reduced them to idiocy; besides, they were taken from those deathlike cells each year, and subjected to the horrible torture of the rack, which often dislocated their joints or crushed their bones, and all this perhaps for merely uttering a sentiment averse to some political party in power! The soldiers and officers also of the Bastile, except the governor, were prisoners in everything but in name. When they entered the walls of that prison, it was for the term of their lives, and a wish expressed even to go out, was instant death. Newgate would not in any respect, bear a similtude to the Bastile. Indeed, the treatment of the prisoners and discipline of the guard was often too lenient, although for disobedience, punishment was sometimes inflicted in the severest manner. The criminals confined here after the year 1800, varied in number from forty-five to sixty, but in 1827, upon their removal to Wethersfield, they numbered one hundred and twenty-seven.

Daily Routine.

A description of the daily management at Newgate, will at this day be found both interesting and amusing. The hatches were opened and the prisoners called out of their dungeon each morning at daylight, and three were ordered to "heave up" at a time; a guard followed the three to their shops, placing them at their work, and chaining those to the block whose tempers were thought to require it. All were brought out likewise in squads of three, and each followed by a guard. To those who never saw the operation, their appearance cannot be truly conceived, as they vaulted forth from the dungeon in their blackness, their chains clanking at every step, and their eyes flashing fire upon the bystanders. It resembled, perhaps more than anything, the belching from the bottomless pit. After a while their rations for the day were carried to them in their several shops. They consisted for each day of one pound of beef or three-fourths of a pound of pork, one pound of bread, one bushel of potatoes for each fifty rations, and one pint of cider to every man. Each one divided his own rations to suit himself—some cooked over their own mess in a small kettle at their leisure, while others disregarding ceremonies, seized their allowance and ate it on an anvil or block. The scene was really graphic, and might remind one of a motley company of foreign emigrants on the deck of a canal-boat, during their visit to the Far West. They were allowed to swap rations, exchange commodities, barter, buy, and sell, at their pleasure. Some would swap their rations for cider, and often would get so tipsy that they could not work, and would "reel to and fro like a drunken man." "Old Guinea," an aged convict, was frequently commissioned by them to go abroad and purchase the *good creature* for them, and would often return laden with two or three gallons. Sometimes, by taking his pay out of the cargo on the road rather freely, his ship would get becalmed, when he would cast anchor by the wayside for the night, making the consignees doubly glad upon his safe arrival "in the beautiful morning." Lieutenant Viet's tavern, a few rods from the prison, was an especial accommodation, not only for travellers, but for the better sort of convicts. He who could muster the needful change, would prevail on some one of the guard to escort him over the way to the inn of the merry old gentleman, where his necessities and those of his escort were amply supplied at the bar. Many an unfortunate fellow, after his release from bondage, has "cast a longing look behind" to the old temple of Bacchus, and appreciated the sentiment of the poet:

> "Of joys departed never to return,
> How painful the remembrance."

All were allowed to work for themselves or others after their daily tasks were finished, and in that way some of them actually laid up considerable sums of money. A little cash, or some choice bits of food from people in the neighborhood, procured many a nice article of cabinet ware, a good basket, a gun repaired by the males, or a knit pair of stockings by the female convicts. The writer, when a boy, was often rewarded for a pocketful of fruit with miniature ships, boxes, brass rings, bow and arrows, and the like; all being more valuable for having been made at Newgate, and all showing the particular branch or handicraft to which each had been accustomed. During the day the guard was changed once in two hours, at the sound of a horn, and in the night a guard entered the caverns every hour and a half, and counted the prisoners. The punishments inflicted for offences and neglect of duty were severe flogging, confinement in stocks in the dungeon, being fed on bread and water during the time, double or treble sets of irons, hanging by the heels, &c., all tending to inflame their revenge and hatred, and seldom were appeals made to their reason or better feelings. Most of them were placed together in the night; solitary lodging, as practiced at this day, being regarded as a punishment, rather than a blessing to them.

Their employment consisted in making nails, barrels, shoes, wagons, doing job-work, farming, and working on the tread-mill. A building for a tread-mill was erected, about the year 1824, for the purpose of grinding grain for prison use, and occasionally for the neighboring inhabitants. A large wheel, between twenty and thirty feet long, was furnished with horizontal flanges as steps, upon which the prisoners trod, and their weight causing the wheel to revolve, furnished the motive power to propel the machinery. Of all labor required of the prisoners, the tread-mill was dreaded the most, and the most stubborn were put to this employment. In extreme cases, one of the *lady birds* was put on the wheel among the men as a punishment, and that was generally sufficient to subdue the most refractory in a very short space of time.* The tread-mill proved however, to be an unprofitable investment for the State.

The following is from Kendall's Travels in the Northern Parts of the United States. He visited Newgate prison in 1807, and says:

"On being admitted into the gaol yard, I found a sentry under arms within the gate, and eight soldiers drawn up in a line in front of the gaoler's house. A bell summoning the prisoners to work had already rung; and in a few moments they began to make their appearance. They came in irregular numbers, sometimes two or three together, and sometimes a single one alone; but whenever one or more were about to cross the yard to the smithery, the soldiers were ordered to present, in readiness to fire. The prisoners were heavily ironed, and secured both by handcuffs and fetters; and being therefore unable to walk, could only make their way by a sort of jump or a hop. On entering the smithery, some went to the sides of the forges, where collars, dependent by iron chains from the roof, were fastened round their necks, and others were chained in pairs to wheelbarrows.† The number of prisoners was about forty; and when they were all disposed of in the manner described, sentries were placed within the buildings which contained them. After viewing thus far the economy of this prison, I left it, proposing to visit the cells at a later hour.

---

*Female convicts were formerly sent to the county jails, but **a law was afterwards passed** authorizing their commitment to Newgate.

† Only the most dangerous and refractory were thus heavily ironed.

"This establishment, as I have said, is designed to be, from all its arrangements, an object of terror; and everything is accordingly contrived to make the life endured in it as burdensome and miserable as possible. In conformity with this idea, the place chosen for the prison is no other than the mouth of a forsaken copper-mine, of which the excavations are employed as cells. They are descended by a shaft, which is secured by a trap-door, within the prison-house, or gaoler's house, which stands upon the mine.

"The trap-door being lifted up, I went down an iron ladder, perpendicularly fixed to the depth of about fifty feet. From the foot of the ladder a rough, narrow, and low passage descends still deeper, till it terminates at a well of clear water, over which is an air-shaft, seventy feet in height, and guarded at its mouth, which is within the gaol yard, by a hatch of iron. The cells are near the well, but at different depths beneath the surface, none perhaps exceeding sixty feet. They are small, rugged, and accommodated with wooden berths, and some straw. The straw was wet, and there was much humidity in every part of this obscure region; but I was assured I ought to attribute this only to the remarkable wetness of the season; that the cells were in general dry, and that they were not found unfavorable to the health of the prisoners.

"Into these cells the prisoners are dismissed at four o'clock in the afternoon, every day without exception, and at all seasons of the year. They descend in their fetters and handcuffs, and at four o'clock in the morning they ascend the iron ladder, climbing it as well as they can by the aid of their fettered limbs. It is to be observed that no women are confined here; the law providing that female convicts, guilty of crimes of which men are to be confined in Newgate prison, are to be sent only to the county gaols.

"Going again into the workshop or smithery, I found the attendants of the prison delivering pickled pork for dinner of the prisoners. Pieces were given separately to the parties at each forge. They were thrown upon the floor, and left to be washed and boiled in the water used for cooling the iron wrought at the forges. Meat had been distributed in like manner for breakfast. The food of the prison is regulated for each day in the week; and consists in an alternation of pork, beef, and peas, with which last no flesh-meat is allowed. Besides the caverns or excavations below, and the gaoler's house above, there are other apartments prepared for the prisoners, and particularly a hospital, of which the neatness and airiness afford a strong contrast to the other parts of the prison. It was also satisfactory to find that in this hospital there were no sick.

"Such is the seat and the scene of punishment provided by Connecticut for criminals not guilty of murder, treason, or either of a few other capital offences. What judgment the reader will pass upon it I do not venture to anticipate; but for myself, I cannot get rid of the impression, that without any extraordinary cruelty in its actual operation, there is something very like cruelty in the device and design."

Escapes and Insurrections.

The following is a relation of other escapes and insurrections, which occurred at various periods in Newgate prison, during a period of nearly forty years.

In November, 1794, a convict by the name of Newel escaped from the prison by digging out. It was the practice at that time to allow the prisoners the choice of lodging in the stone cellar under the guard-room (generally known by the name of the stone jug), or of going from thence down into the caverns. During the night a noise below was heard by the guard, and some of them went down among the prisoners to learn the cause, but could discover nothing out of place. In the morning on counting them, as was customary, one was discovered to be missing. It was found that the prisoners, in some unaccountable manner, had contrived to loosen and pull out one of the large cubic stones on the bottom of the cellar. Through the aperture thus made, they hauled out the earth, pouring it down the shaft, and incredible as it may seem, they dug a hole through gravel, earth, and stones, under the floor and wall large enough for a man to crawl out! It appears that when the guard went down among them in the night, the prisoners could hear their arrangements for descending, and instantly replaced the stone and prevented a discovery of their operations. Newel, being a very small man, was the only one who succeeded in making his escape; he was never retaken.

In the year 1802 the prisoners rose upon the guard. The commander, Colonel Thomas Sheldon, was then sick, and soon after died; all the officers and guard were sick also, except Mr. Dan Forward, a private. With occasional assistance of people in the neighborhood, the entire charge of the prisoners, at that time amounting to between thirty and forty, devolved upon him. They had heard that many of the officers and privates were sick, and observing that one man performed nearly the whole duty, their suspicions were confirmed, and their plot strengthened. It is not certain whether there was a fair understanding among them; if there was, their courage most miserably failed. While they were passing down into their caverns at the close of the day as usual, and, when nearly all of them were going down the ladder, those who remained refused to proceed, and began an attack upon Forward, who was standing near. He was a robust, stout fellow, over six feet high, and always ready for any contest; and instead of retreating, he returned their compliments, taking one by the neck and another by the heels, and dashing them down into the shaft upon the rest, who had now begun to come up. The neighbors hearing a scuffle at the prison, ran over to his assistance; but their aid was unnecessary, as Forward had vanquished his foes and turned their course into the dungeon. It is very likely that all could have escaped if Forward had betrayed the least sign of fear, or had resorted to any other mode of persuasion.

At this time a very contagious fever raged at the prison, and soon began to spread among the convicts. It was without doubt owing to the filth in and around the prison, and to the want of care and attention to their cleanliness and comfort. The disease was so virulent, that in order to arrest its progress, a barn was engaged of Captain Roswell Phelps, into which they were to be removed. People in the vicinity were employed to take care of the sick and perform the duties of guard; but all the prisoners except three Irishmen being sick, it was found impracticable to remove, and after some weeks the disease abated. None of the prisoners, however, died, and no other instance of a general contagion among them ever occurred.

In 1806, on the 1st of November, a rebellion took place which for its results deserves notice. About thirty prisoners in the nail-shop had procured keys made from the pewter buttons on their clothes, and with those keys they were to unlock their fetters. It was agreed that one of their number should strike a shovel across a chimney, and that was to be the signal for them all to unlock fetters, and commence an attack upon the guard, to wrest their weapons from them and use them to the best advantage. The signal was given, their fetters were unlocked, and two of their number began the attack. Aaron Goomer, a negro, and another, seized an officer by the name of Smith, who not having time to draw his sword, struck upon them with scabbard and all, breaking his sword, and while the scuffle was going on, a guard named Roe ran to the spot with his musket, and levelling it at Goomer, shot him dead on the spot. Two balls passed through his head, his hair was singed, and his brains scattered round the shop. His comrade seeing his fate, returned to his post. The courage of the rest "oozed out at their 'fingers' ends,'" for not one of them dared to stir from their places, although their shackles were unfastened. Had a well-concerted attack been made and sustained by the rebels at this moment, they would have commanded the prison in five minutes, and could have put to death every officer and private in their quarters.

Three brothers by the name of Barnes, natives of North Haven, were imprisoned together for the crime of burglary, in 1803. These were the most active and finest-looking men in the prison. They were very ingenious and adroit, and could construct almost any mechanism required of them. These were the fellows who planned the insurrection before spoken of, and they made the pewter keys for unlocking the fetters. They were experienced in making keys, and could once, it is said, open any store in New Haven; but their ingenuity at length brought them to an unfortunate place.

The fact is surprising that the same three committed the same offence again, and were convicted and imprisoned again just three years after! These brothers were regarded by the officers as extremely dangerous, and for various offences in the prison, they were kept bound with two sets of fetters during the day, and also chained to the block, besides being sometimes chained by their necks to a beam overhead, and at night they were put into the dungeons, and their feet made fast in stocks.

One of the convicts named Parker, had been famous for counterfeiting the character of priest. He had been known to have many violent attacks of pretended piety, generally appropriating to himself the name and office of an unordained minister, a part which he managed with a great deal of dexterity, and commonly without suspicion on the part of his dear hearers, that he was an impostor. His exhortations had been terrible to all stony hearts, and where his preaching lacked mental light or logic, he always had ready a supply of bombast and bodily contortions.

Another game it is said he performed to admiration. When he could hear of the absence of a long-lost friend in a family, he would appear and claim the identical relationship himself, and act all the tragedy or romantic pathos of a joyful return.

In one instance he claimed to be the stray husband of a disconsolate woman, and was received by her with all the attachment supposable at such a happy reunion. His real identity was not discovered until in taking off his shoes, the lady remarked that he possessed more toes than belonged to him—her husband having lost one by amputation; he replied with ready adroitness that the lost toe *had grown out again* since his long absence. This determined the question as to his identity, and he at once received such a summary ejectment, as is best administered by a woman of sensible spirit.

How astonishing such adroitness!—to be preacher and " steal the livery of Heaven to serve the devil in;" to be brother, son, or husband, appearing more natural, so to speak, in a fictitious garb, than in his real character! When his term of service expired, and as he was passing out of the prison gate, one of the convicts exclaimed, " Wo to the inhabitants of the earth, for the devil has gone out among them."

Prince Mortimer, a prisoner, lived to a very advanced age. He died at the prison in Wethersfield, in 1834, supposed to be 110 years old; he commonly went by the name of Guinea, which was probably given to him on account of his native country. His complexion did not in the least belie his name, for surely he was the personification of " darkness visible." His life was a tale of misfortunes, and his fate won the commiseration of all who knew him. He was captured on the coast of Guinea by a slaver when a boy; was transported in a filthy slave-ship to Connecticut, then a slave colony, and was sold to one of the Mortimer family in

Middletown. He was a servant to different officers in the Revolutionary War; had been sent on errands by General Washington, and said he had "straddled many a cannon when fired by the Americans at the British troops." For the alleged crime of poisoning his master he was doomed to Newgate prison, in 1811, for life. He appeared a harmless, clever old man, and as his age and infirmities rendered him a burden to the keepers, they frequently tried to induce him to quit the prison. Once he took his departure, and after rambling around in search of some one he formerly knew, like the aged prisoner released from the Bastile, he returned to the gates of the prison, and begged to be re-admitted to his dungeon home, and in prison ended his unhappy years!

Samuel Smith, alias Samuel Corson, a native of New Hampshire, while confined at Newgate for passing counterfeit money, wrote an account of his own life, which was published in 1826. He stated many queer circumstances about himself, and the various paths of crime which he had followed through life. It appears he had been a recruiting officer in the service, and was stationed at Plattsburg, N. Y. One of his pranks is worthy of being recorded in his own words:—

"One evening, I, together with a number of non-commissioned officers, took a walk down town for our amusement, and on our return home, I saw by a light through a window of a Mr. I's house, something laying very carefully rolled up, on a table under the window. I also perceived that there was no person in the room. I now thinking to get something rare and fresh, in order for our suppers, lifted up the window, and on putting my hand in, felt by its ribs and size, enough to convince me that it was a good *roaster*, and I of course made it a lawful prize. Putting it under my coat, I said nothing about it to my comrades, until our arrival at my quarters, where I invited them to accept of some refreshment. After taking a light and introducing a good bottle of brandy, I thought it the most convenient time to uncover my booty, in order to satisfy our craving appetites. At this moment, all eyes were gazing at the mysterious prize, when lo! to my utter suprise and astonishment, it had turned from a *roaster* to a (dead) *colored child*. You can hardly imagine, dear readers, what were my feelings at this critical moment, not only from exposition among my fellow-officers, nor disappointment in my intended and contemplated supper, but also in the thoughts of robbing some unhappy parents of their darling child. I need not add, that they had a hearty fit of laughter, at my expense, whilst my wits were all at work in order to devise some manner of getting out of the hobble, and restoring the infant undiscovered, to its proper owners. This I thought best to do, by returning it immediately to Mr. I's house, and in order to accomplish this, I took it again under my coat and repaired to the main guard, to obtain liberty to return to the village. On asking Lieutenant Ellison (who was officer of the guard) he discovered something white hanging below my coat, and insisted on knowing what it was; when I had of course to reveal the whole secret to him; he also laughed heartily and told me to go on. When I returned to Mr. I's, the house was filled with both men and women, who, having missed the child, did not know what to think of its mysterious flight. I had at first thought of leaving it at the door, but fearing the numerous hogs in the vicinity would destroy it, I altered my mind, and taking it by the heels threw it into the room among them. At this crisis, how must they have felt, to see it re-appear amongst them, and feeling at the same time, the effects of innumerable particles of glass, which flew in all directions over the room. Their screams were indescribable—by which, in a few moments, not only the house, but the street was filled with astonished spectators; all anxious to know what was the matter. On my return home, I met many repairing to the house, and on some of them inquiring what was the matter up the street, I told them that I believed there was a crazy man in the house of Mr. I. On arriving at the barracks all was still, and I heard nothing more respecting it for some days."

A convict, by the name of Newman, was a noted prison-breaker. Although he perhaps could not boast of unlocking, scaling, and digging out of so many prisons as the famous Stephen Burrows, yet his character, as it was written, compared very well. He escaped in various ways from several prisons in Canada and the United States, but this one, he said, "was the hardest and most secure prison he ever entered." However, he contrived several plans for escaping; once he feigned himself to be dead. He was accordingly laid out as a corpse, and preparations made for his interment; but before finding his carcass firmly under ground, he concluded it best to have his resurrection, and at length ventured to disclose to his attendants the important fact, that he would feel quite as comfortable in his long home, if he could get the breath out of his body and make his heart stop beating. He often pretended to have fits, requiring medical aid, and what was of more consequence, the aid of a little Brandy or Madeira. He pretended to raise blood from his lungs whenever he wished to draw sympathy from the guard, until it was discovered that it was a substance made to order by chewing pieces of *red brick*, or pricking his gums. He would vary his pulse by pounding his elbows and other violent means, and thus deceive the physician. He said he could reduce his flesh in ten days by sucking a copper cent in his mouth each night, and swallowing the saliva, which destroys the juices of the body, and produces premature decay. He was continually apprehensive that he would yet be taken back to England, where he said he should have to answer for the crime of murder, as a thousand pounds reward for his arrest stood against him. His chief desire was to avoid labor at the nail-block, but he was finally cured of his tricks with the threat of having the brand of *rogue* set on his forehead.

A GRAVE SUBJECT.

A comical episode took place one day upon the death of a negro convict, named Charles Mears. His body was placed in a roughly made box, as was the practice, and two prisoners, and a guard by the name of Moses Talcott, were detailed to convey the body to a secluded spot half a mile north, where the prisoners were usually buried. Before the box and contents were taken in charge by the *grave* cortege, another convict, a white man, whose name is not now recalled, considering that "even exchange is no robbery," slyly took off the cover from the box, and pulling out the dead negro hid him in a bye corner, depositing his own live carcass therein. At the appointed hour the aforesaid bearers took up their *grave* subject, and followed by the guard, soon arrived at the place of burial. They set down their load and were about to commit "dust to dust and ashes to ashes," when to their utter consternation, a strange sepulchral noise was heard from within that coffin. They listened for a moment transfixed with horror, and the next moment all fled with the utmost speed back to the prison and related their horrible adventure.

It is needless to relate that the *live* corpse who made "from the tombs a doleful sound," being well satisfied with his ingenious ruse, took a lively departure and was never re-taken. The rightful occupant of the box was at length discovered, and the aforesaid attendants with more caution and less confidence, deposited their charge in safety, while all parties considered the affair as a *grave* subject in more respects than one.

It was frequently customary for farmers and others in the neighborhood to employ the prisoners in their fields, being accompanied at such times by some of the guard. They also performed a great amount of labor in quarrying stone for the prison buildings, and other uses. Six of them on one occasion were sent out a short distance to quarry stone, in charge of one officer and two privates. With no fetters, and a fair field before them, they perceived the chance a good one for escape. Their plan was to get their keepers near together, to employ their attention about some trifle, and quickly seize their arms. Accordingly they persuaded their keepers to peel off some birch bark and make caps for them, and while the cap business was going on, and the attention of the *cap makers* was occupied in their vocation, their weapons were seized in an instant; the refugees, dividing the spoils and forming themselves into squads, quickly scampered over hills. The forlorn guards retreated to the prison, told their sad tale to the captain, and at once received their discharge. The prisoners were all re-taken; some in the western part the State for stealing; the others stole a boat in the Connecticut river, and steering down the stream leisurely, were captured in East Hartford meadows.

The wit of some of the convicts is well illustrated in an anecdote of one of them, an Irishman named Dublin. He was at his work making nails, when at one time Major Humphrey, who then commanded, came along, and said to him, "Dublin, your nails are defective; the heads are not made alike." "Ah," said he, "Major, if our heads had all been made alike, faith, I should not have been caught here." Dublin afterwards tried to escape by leaping over the paling. He succeeded in getting upon the top, and in leaping down, one of the iron spikes with which the enclosure was mounted, caught in his fetters and turned him, as he said, "tother end up." For some time he hung suspended, head downwards, between heaven and earth, seventeen feet high, until at last, after tearing off his finger ends and nails in his struggles he turned himself back sufficiently to disentangle his feet, when he fell to the ground, and soon scampered away among the swamps and bushes. There he remained until aroused by the unwelcome calls of his stomach, when he ventured out in the night, and opening a window in the neighborhood, he appropriated to himself a good loaf of bread and a cheese, and again hid himself for two days. In trying to break his fetters with a stone, he was overheard by one of the guard, Michael Holcomb, who called to him, "Dublin, what are doing?" "I am driving the sheep out of my pasture," said he. "But Dublin you must come along with me." "Faith, Misthur Holcomb, surely this is not me," replied Dublin. He was taken to the prison, where Holcomb received the reward of ten dollars which had been offered.

In the spring of 1822, there was a rebellion of a very serious nature. In the fall previous, between thirty and forty criminals were added to the number in prison, and this reinforcement was composed of rough and hard characters. This increase was in consequence of legislative enactments transferring many from the county jails, which were all constructed of wood, and very insecure. The terms of sentence were mostly long, which served to fire them with desperation. The same fall a plot was set on foot by them for an outbreak, but it was discovered and defeated. The next spring they perfected their plans of operation in a most masterly manner. The insurgents comprised the whole number in the prison, amounting to more than one hundred. Their force was stronger than ever before, and the number of guards less, being at the time only seventeen. The captain, Tuller, was absent through the night, also one sergeant, one private, and the cook. The intention of the rebels was to rise in all the shops, *en masse*, at a given signal to knock down the officers, take their weapons, and get possession of the guard-house where the arms were kept, and then to take sole command of the works. The signal was given in the nail-shop by a blow from a shovel, and officer Roe was instantly knocked down senseless with a bar of iron. They seized his cutlass, and attacked a guard; but so many were engaged upon him at once, pulling different ways, that they did not succeed in getting his musket. Officer Case in the meantime stationed a sentinel at the door of the guard-room, with a loaded musket and bayonet charged, which being noticed by the prisoners in the other shops, prevented their advancing to the attack, and seemed to dishearten them at once. The bold rebels in the nail-shop kept up the struggle, and sledges, spikes, and other missiles flew in all directions, and confusion and uproar reigned throughout. At this critical moment officer Griswold arrived at the prison, and proceeded directly to the scuffle at the musket. He drew his pistol, fired upon and wounded a prisoner. Roe by this time had come to his senses; he arose from the ground and shot another, when presently several guards presented their cocked muskets, which immediately quelled the assailants. The general cry of the prisoners was now for quarter: "Spare us! Don't kill us!—don't kill us!" The captain soon arrived, and bound the ringleaders in double irons.

Ephraim Shaylor, one of the guard, was sent out to accompany two prisoners, an Indian and a white man, about 1½ miles from the prison, where they were employed in reaping. At the close of the day, on their return, the prisoners requested permission to gather some apples and carry them home, to which Shaylor consented; he also was engaged in picking them up, when they sprang upon his back, crushed him down, and secured his weapons, a cutlass and fowling-piece. One of them took a large stone and was about to smash out his brains, but the other dissented, and they concluded it best to take him to a copse of bushes near by and there dispatch him. One followed at his back, holding him by his sword-belt with cutlass in hand, and the other marched at a respectable distance, with musket charged, in true military style, and onward they marched towards the fatal spot. Our hero now concluded that his fatal hour had come, and thought if he must die, there might be at least a choice in the mode; and considering that a shot in the back at such a crisis would be no dishonor. On a sudden he slipped the belt over his head and made for the prison, while the victors were disputing between themselves which should take the musket and fire upon him. Shaylor reached the prison in safety, rallied several others and pursued them, but they were not to be found.

After their victory, it appears that the Indian proposed to the white man to break each other's fetters, to which the other agreed, and after those of the Indian were broken, the crafty liar took speedy leave of his comrade without reciprocating the favor, thus proving that the old adage in this instance, is not true, "there is honor among rogues." The white man secreted himself in the mountains through the day, and at night went to a blacksmith's shop in Suffield, and with a chisel cut off his fetters. Both were afterwards taken for crime and re-committed to Newgate, where their condition and that of their enemy as victor and vanquished was strangely reversed, and Shaylor had an opportunity of enjoying his right of laying upon their bare backs a few keen lashes. Mr. Shaylor afterwards held a commission in the army, was engaged in the battle of Bridgewater, and was wounded.

It was customary to give the prisoners in each shop a daily take of work, a certain number of pounds of nails, or amount of boot and shoe work, or number of barrels to be made and to be completed by about 3 P. M. each day, after which they were marched into a room built of stone under the guard-house. There they were kept together until evening, when they were required to descend into the caverns for the night; a few, however, were usually employed about the premises during the day as waiters, cooks, etc. After the main body were locked in the stone room, the large gate leading into the yard was unfastened, and left open for admission of teams and for persons who transacted business at the prison.

The following is related by General Hillyer, of Hartford,

being at that time one of the guard. One day a large, powerful negro employed in the cook-room noticing that the guard, Mr. Lott Thompson (a very pious man) was intently reading his Bible, suddenly seized a stick of wood and knocked him senseless to the floor. The negro than ran for the open gate, but fortunately the keeper, Captain Washburne, happened to be returning at the same time, and the negro seeing his plan so unexpectedly frustrated, turned and ran back into a room, and hid himself in a meal chest. The Captain followed and pulled him out, well powdered over with meal, and placed him in irons and close quarters. He was afterwards convicted of the offence, and sentenced to a further term of imprisonment. Mr. Thompson was at length restored to consciousness, but never fully recovered from his injuries.

In contrast with the grim aspect of the dungeons below ground, Newgate witnessed occasionally high carnival *above* ground. The officers and guard with people outside the walls used a room in one of the prison buildings as a dancing hall in the evening, occasionally, where, with the aforesaid hero of the meal-chest as fiddler, they "tripped the light fantastic toe."

A thief by the name of James Smith, a native of Groton, Conn., was imprisoned for horse-stealing, in 1822, for the term of six years. He had been a great counterfeiter, and circumstances which afterwards came to light are evidence that he had been a barbarous pirate. The piratical crew had sailed in a French vessel, and after obtaining much plunder, fearing to enter any port without regular papers, they sunk their vessel on the coast of North Carolina, carried their specie in three boats, and buried it all, except one large trunk full, on the beach in Currituck county. In corroboration of the above it appears that while he was a prisoner in Newgate, he offered David Foster, a guard, $200 if he would assist him to escape, telling him he had a great quantity of specie buried on the coast of North Carolina. Foster refused, but promised to say nothing about it. This he testified in court when afterwards called upon as a witness. Smith in a few months afterwards escaped from prison, as was supposed, by bribery.

The following respecting him is related by Mr. Benjamin Taylor, a planter recently living in North Carolina. Smith and seven or eight others came to his house in the year 1822, and hired of him a room; they employed him with four of his slaves to cross Currituck sound, and obtained a large trunk, very heavy, and returned to his house, where they all remained about one week. While there he saw them divide a large sum of specie among themselves, and Smith, appearing to be at their head, took the largest sum. They were arrested on suspicion of being robbers, but for want of sufficient evidence discharged. They all then left for Norfolk, Va., except Smith, who remained several weeks. During this time he often appeared to be deranged, would talk to himself, and told the servants that he "had made many a man walk the plank overboard." He then went to the north, and was imprisoned at Newgate for stealing a horse. After his escape from prison as above stated, he returned to the house of Mr. Taylor and staid about one week. While there he employed several men in digging on the beach. Their search was fruitless, for the storms and waves had dashed upon the beach too long, and it is supposed swept the treasures into the ocean. He then went away to some place unknown to Mr. Taylor. It now appears from the prison records that he came to Connecticut, where he was taken and again sentenced for twenty-three years on four indictments for horse stealing. His last home on earth was in prison, and there he died in 1836.

The following sad misfortune which happened to one of the convicts has afforded material for several absurd and exaggerated tales, fabricated about the old prison:—

An old negro, named Jake, a shoemaker, accused of burning his leather, was shackled and put into a dark cell in the cavern used for solitary confinement. This small room was partitioned off with a thick wall and a strong plank and iron door. It was, and is now known as the "sounding-room;" and if the visitor is curious as to the origin of the term, let him sing or speak in a full bass tone and he will be surprised at the loud, sepulchral reverberations. Here refractory prisoners were confined in solitude, chained to a heavy ring and staple in the rock, and fed on bread and water until subdued. The negro, as appears by his own story, busy with tricks and experiments in his solitude, pulled his fetters from their proper position on his ankles up over the calves of his legs, innocently supposing that he could push them down again at will. But the venous blood began to accumulate below the iron bands; and his legs were soon so swollen that the fetters could not be pushed down. When the guard went down to carry him his bread he found the negro in great agony. A surgeon was summoned who ascertained that the irons were so embedded in the swollen flesh that they could not be cut, and in order to save his life he was obliged to amputate both his legs. The old fellow survived the operation, and was soon after discharged from prison by order of the legislature—it being quite evident, doubtless, that he had been sufficiently punished, and that he was not left in such a physical condition as to trouble the outside world any more. He used afterwards to labor, in his crippled way, for people in the neighborhood, and was living until a few years ago.

The last tragedy developed at Newgate took place on the night previous to the removal to Wethersfield. Abel N. Starkey, an ingenious criminal, was the victim. He was a native of Roxbury, Mass., was committed in 1824 for twenty years, for the crime of making counterfeit money. By his ingenuity and industry at the prison he had amassed $100 in cash. On the night of September 28th, 1827, being the day previous to the removal of the prisoners to Wethersfield, he requested permission to lodge in the dungeon, which was granted to him. From some cause which has never been explained, the hatch which covered one of the wells communicating with the cavern, was unfastened. During the night he laid hold of the well-rope and ascended upon it part of the way up, when it broke and precipitated him into the water, and a bucket fell upon his head; the noise was heard above, and he was found dead. His feet were tied together with a handkerchief for the purpose, as is supposed, of assisting him in climbing the rope. Only $50 were found in his possession; the balance was probably the price paid to some confederate for unfastening the hatch.

It would seem that Newgate prison, in the course of its duration, had contained all which was various in character, determined in crime, and deep in degradation. It compassed all ages, from boyhood to extreme old age; both sexes, colors, and different occupations; students from college, and others unable to read or write. Those skilled in phrenology might have had a rich treat in exploring the bumps on some of those hard heads, and the solving of their characteristics would have afforded amusement and perhaps instruction.

Seriously, it is difficult to account for the wayward inclination of some of them, especially those who were imprisoned a number of times, and for the same kind of offence each term, unless it can be accounted for on phrenological principles. It may be said to indicate only a depraved heart, but a depraved heart must have a strange kind of head to run repeatedly into the same crime and get back to the same prison. But I leave it to those who understand the science to defend the ground, presuming that the truth of their cause will insure them a triumphant issue.

When the number and difference of characters kept in that prison is considered, and the treatment which they received is appreciated, it will at once be seen how unavailing the system must have been for their security or their reformation. The custom of fastening their feet to bars of iron to which chains were attached from their necks, chaining them to the block, and likewise to a beam above, while at their work, scourging their bodies like beasts, &c., taught them to look upon themselves in a measure as they were looked upon by others, objects of dread, and possessing characters more like fiends than men. With such treatment, reformation must have been, and was, entirely out of the question. The system was very well suited to turn men into devils, but it never could transform devils into men. Instead of putting them in cells separately at night, where they might have opportunity for reflection, they were suffered to congregate together, good and bad, young and old to brew mischief, and to teach new vices to those unpracticed. Their midnight revels, as may be supposed, were often like the howling in a pandemonium of tigers, banishing sleep and forbidding rest.

It is not desired that these remarks, however, should be so construed as to impute blame to the officers or guard of the prison. Although they were many times in fault, still, as the prison was constructed, and in the way that service was required of them, it was impossible to preserve that degree of order and discipline so essential to success. They had no approved system of prison discipline to study, no correct views of punishment connected with reformation were at that day generally known, and but few branches of business were thought of, which would yield a fair compensation and save the State expense.

The insecurity of Newgate prison, and the constant burden upon the treasury of the State for its support, excited a very strong discussion in the public prints, and in the legislature, for several years. The subject of a new prison on a more modern plan, and the abandonment of the old one raised a powerful party in its support. Among the foremost in this enterprise was Martin Welles, Esq., of Wethersfield, who labored zealously for its accomplishment. The proprosition was opposed by others living in the vicinity of Newgate, among whom was Major Orson P. Phelps, an enterprising contractor, who had furnished the prison with beef, and other necessaries. The Major indulged his ready poetic wit, on one occasion, by the following sentiment:

> "O'er the dark side on Copper hill,
> *Martin Welles* has stopped their treading mill.
> 'Tis ten to one if he don't miss it,
> For Doctor *Buck* can't deal out physic."

He was well answered by the author of another couplet:

> "Say what you will, old Newgate helps
> The beef contractor, Major Phelps.

The following song was composed by Dr. Eliphalet Buck, and sung on the occasion of completing the walls of Newgate prison in 1802. Dr. Buck was for many years the established physician for Newgate, and was a complete embodiment of fun as well as physic, but had not made the art of poetry a study, evidently:

> Attend, all ye villains, that live in the state,
> Consider the walls that encircle Newgate,
>   Your place of abode, if justice were done.
> The assembly in wisdom, when they did behold
> The first wooden pickets, grown ruined and old,
> They granted a sum to the wise overseers,
> Which, amply sufficient to make the repairs,
>   And they did decide to repair with hewn stone.
>
> In the year one thousand eight hundred and two,
>   A party collected, to split and to hew.
> Their names in my song, shall last with the wall;
> First, Lieutenant Barber the job undertakes;
> Beneath his strong labor, old Copper Hill shakes,
> With his workmen in order, the stone for to square,
> And others strong burdens with cheerfulness bear,
>   While each one delights to attend to his call.
>
> The next in the column is sage Pettibone,
> Whose skill in the work is exceeded by none.
>   To handle the gravel, or poise the great maul;
> With him senior Jared an equal part bears,
> And in the hard labor he equally shares:
> While Gillett, and Holcomb, and Cosset appear,
> And Hillyer all anxious the fabric to rear,
>   To lay the foundation—to strengthen the Wall.
>
> Bold Harrington, Goddard, and Lieutenant Reed,
> Each lend their assistance the work to proceed.
>   Perhaps there are others, whose names I don't call,
> With hammers, and chisels, and crowbars and gads,
> And Wanrax, with other poor prisoner lads,
> To hand up the mortar, or carry the hod;
> Which may, to some strangers appear very odd,
>   To think the poor culprits help build their own Wall.
>
> November the tenth, for the good of the state,
> They finished the wall and completed the gate,
>   Which for numerous years may swing and not fall.
> Then each one returns to his sweetheart or wife,

With plenty of cash to support them in life
With joy and gladness for what they had done,
In hewing and squaring, and laying the stone,
Not wholly unmindful of building the Wall.

Now here's to the landlord, before that we go,
We wish him success, and his lady also,
  For their kind assistance to great and to small,
For the benefit had from his plentiful bar,
And the free intercourse which produces no jar;
To him and his neighbors, and every good man,
Who always we've wanted to lend us a hand
  To drive on the work, and finish the Wall.

Now last, to the prisoners, we make this remark,
Who are left to the keeping of Commodore Clark.
  It may be of service, to one and to all,
Repine not too much, though your lot may seem hard,
You've a judicious keeper, and well-disposed guard;
If you behave well you have nothing to dread—
You've beef, pork, and sauce, and a plenty of bread,
  So behave well, and get the outside of the Wall.

Some of the prisoners were made to assist in building the wall, and it appears that they were permitted to participate in the jollification after it was completed. An Irish prisoner, named Patrick, offered upon the occasion the following toast:

"Here's to Lieutenant Barber's great wall—May it be like the walls of Jericho, and *tumble down at the sound of a ram's horn.*"

The toast given by Dublin was equally sarcastic, viz:

"Here's health to the Captain and all the rest of the prisoners."

During the fifty-four years in which Newgate was used as a prison, fourteen persons had held the office of overseer, viz: Erastus Wolcott, Josiah Bissell, Jonathan Humphrey, Asahel Holcomb, James Forward, Matthew Griswold, Roger Newberry, John Treadwell, Pliny Hillyer, Samuel Woodruff, Martin Sheldon, Reuben Barker, Jonathan Pettibone, Jr., Thomas K. Brace. *Keepers:*—John Viets, Peter Curtis, Reuben Humphreys, Thomas Sheldon, Salmon Clark, Charles Washburn, Elam Tuller, Alexander H. Griswold, Andrew Denison.

CONNECTICUT STATE PRISON.

The present penitentiary of Connecticut is situated on the margin of a beautiful cove in the town of Wethersfield, about three miles from Hartford, and is regarded as a penitentiary of the first order. Its location, its construction, its financial management and discipline, have won the admiration of every State in the Union. It has proved to the world that criminal punishment can be made a safeguard to society, a protection to the honest industry of the people, and also a benefit to the moral and physical condition of the convicts. The prison limits comprise about one and a half acres of ground, which is enclosed by a wall of hard sandstone, 18 feet high, 3 feet thick at its base, and inclining to $1\frac{1}{3}$ feet at the top. Within and adjoining this wall, are buildings of the same material, and of brick, used as the warden's apartment, hospital, and chapel, and for workshops and cells. In the yard is a cistern underground, for water, of the capacity of 100 hogsheads. Water is also brought to the prison in pipes from Hartford. Gas made at the prison is used to light the premises.

A portion of the cell building is whitewashed with lime each day, which purifies the air, and gives to the lodging apartments an appearance of neatness. Most of the convicts enjoy that blessing of punishment, a separate cell at night, but the largely increased number of late (now 264) requires more room for proper accommodation. No one is allowed while at work to look at any visitor, or to catch the eye of his fellow, but all are intent upon the business before them.

A library of suitable books, comprising about 1400 volumes, is provided for such as can read, and those who cannot are instructed by the chaplain, who is assisted occasionally by the warden and other officers. The library is highly prized by the convicts, who spend many of their solitary hours in reading, and the benefits have been so apparent, that the State has usually appropriated annually $200 for the purchase of books for their use. Male convicts are employed at present in the manufacture of mechanics' tools, boot and shoe and cigar making. The females are under the charge of a matron, and are employed in making and mending clothes, and in general laundry work. The services of most of the male convicts are let by the warden to companies or contractors, who pay monthly a stipulated price per day for the services of each prisoner, and no able-bodied person is exempt from labor. Reverses in business and other causes occasionally vary the net income in all penitentiaries, but the net profits of the State prison at Wethersfield have usually averaged about $2000 per annum, while most other State prisons show a large annual indebtedness.

It is interesting to observe how much depends in the success of a prison, upon skill and discipline in its management. For seventeen years previous to the removal of the prison, in 1827, the average annual tax upon the State treasury for the support of Newgate, including buildings and repairs, was over $7000. The present institution has paid for all its buildings and fixtures, and seventeen acres of land. It paid $7000 dollars to the counties of the State, for the erection of county jails on the improved penitentiary system, and $7000 to the school districts in the State for school apparatus, thus causing ignorance and crime to help to educate the rising generation.

Strict order and discipline are apparent in every department, and yet without any vain show of power. No bars or fetters are worn by the prisoners; no armed sentinel is seen, except upon the two towers; no muskets, swords, or pistols are carried daily within the walls, and only within the guard-room are any weapons of death to be seen. The prison force consists of the warden, deputy warden, matron, six watchmen, and eight overseers for the shops—which latter are usually paid by the contractors.

Health of the Convicts.

By the reports of the prison physicians for several years past, and the remarkably small number usually under treatment in the hospital, its appears that this prison, from its excellent hygienic management, ranks high in respect of its healthfulness. The directors in their report say, "The average health of the prisoners has been better, in fact, than an average equal number of the inhabitants of the surrounding towns."

In all penitentiaries there are criminals possessing strange and unaccountable characteristics; but whatever their general propensities, they are influenced by one motive while in the prison, which is common to all of them, and that is a desire to escape from confinement. But the Connecticut penitentiary has furnished one singular exception to this general rule, or rather the rule has been transposed in one singular case. A young female named Abby Jane was committed in 1853 for the term of four years, for the crime of horse-stealing. She served out her term, was duly discharged, and presented with her former articles of clothing, etc.; and with the present then usually given to all at their departure. of two dollars in money. She soon after obtained employment at housework in the neighborhood, and for a while appeared to behave herself well; but at length her former habit of thieving predominated, and some of her pilfering was detected by the family. Abby took her leave, but soon privately returned, and stealing a horse-blanket from General Welles, living near by, she ensconced herself under his barn floor, which she appropriated as her lodging apartment, with the stolen blanket for her coverlid. Here she lived for several days, subsisting upon whatever plunder she could get, and by milking the cows in the neighborhood in the night, retreating each day to her kennel under the barn.

But the remembrance of prison life had such fascinating charms, that she contrived a plan to scale the walls, and get into the prison, by climbing a tree which stood near. She leaped down from the top of the wall into the yard of the female apartment, and secreted herself among the rubbish in the wood-pile. Her female cronies, surprised and gratified to enjoy again the company of their cunning visitor, clandestinely supplied her with food, whenever they found opportunity. In this manner she lived four or five days, thieving whenever she could, and finally took up her lodging in an old ash-hole, or oven. The matron had missed provisions and other articles, and was puzzled to account for the loss. A general search was made, when the warden, on removing some pieces of refuse stove-pipe under the oven, discovered the once fair face of Abby, peering through the sooty canopy, and she was again in the clutches of the law. No one, however, seemed willing to indict her for the novel crime of breaking *into* a prison, and she was sentenced for *theft* to the county jail for one year. There she served out her time and was released, but soon after she broke into a dwelling, and appropriated to herself a pair of pantaloons, containing in the pockets $500, besides other articles, for which she was again committed to Hartford jail. After her term had expired, the jailor, relying on her earnest promises of reformation, sent her into the country to his father's house, for employment. But there, true to her propensity, she again began to steal and was consequently discharged. As to her whereabouts afterwards report says not.

SOME OF THE NOTORIOUS CONVICTS FOR LIFE.

William H. Greene, aged 61, was born in Virginia, and convicted at Litchfield in 1869. He had murdered his wife, and committed other crimes; had been an ordained clergyman, and claimed that he had been at one time a presiding elder of the Methodist church. He had been a political public speaker, possessed of a good education and eloquent oratorical powers. In this man's career the fact is apparent that mere education of the brain, unaccompanied by moral influences, is of little avail in restraining any being from committing crime; and it is a positive error in the management of some of our schools and seminaries that this vital subject is so strangely overlooked.

Lydia Sherman, a female convict, was born in New Jersey, and is 51 years of age. She was convicted at New Haven in 1873, of murder in the second degree. By her own confession she had poisoned *three husbands* and *four of her children*! She seemed to possess a strange monomania for dispatching her nearest relatives, and although admitting that she had always lived pleasantly with them, she claimed "they were better off in the other world than in this one of misery." In her appearance she seemed like a simple, harmless woman, and said she "was in as comfortable a situation as she could reasonably expect." The fact that her family was very poor, and that she had murdered seven of them, probably impressed the jury with the idea that she was partially insane, which induced them to render the singular verdict of murder in the *second degree*.

The annals of crime do not, perhaps, afford a character more remarkable for perversity and desperation than that of a convict by the name of Dave Kentley, *alias* James Wilson and several other *aliases* which he had at various times assumed. This fiend in human form, while in prison, murdered Warden Willard, in 1870.

He was born in Belfast, Ireland, and was 47 years of age when he committed the murder. He said he had never attended school a day in his life; and the return of his parents to Ireland left him here without parental control.

In justification of his propensities he claimed that all boys are born natural thieves and robbers, and only need the opportunity to develop, as he had, their perverse natures. He took his first lessons in crime in a small way, at the Five Points, New York, when ten or twelve years of age; and, connecting himself with other desperadoes, he was afterwards engaged in robberies at Philadelphia, New York New London, Hartford, and some cities at the West.

He had, during his career, escaped from four prisons in different states. In escaping from prison in Michigan, in the winter season, he had frozen both his feet, and was obliged to suffer partial amputation.

In 1851 he was convicted of burglary, and sent to Wethersfield prison for six years; and at the time of the murder was serving his second term for a similar offence. There he made two attempts to escape, but was discovered by Warden Willard; for this he swore vengeance against him. In some way he procured a knife-blade, which he secreted about his person, and which, in his cell on Sunday, he fastened to the end of a cane that had been kindly allowed him on account of his lameness. He then sent for the warden, and requested him to read from a slate on which something was written, and while warden Willard was thus engaged, Wilson stabbed him in the abdomen, inflicting a wound from which he died in about four hours. While in Hartford jail, during his trial for this murder, he tried to escape, and also made an attempt to jump from the wagon, on the way to the courthouse.

Upon his trial he made an able speech to the jury in self-defence. He wrote a long petition to the General Assembly for commutation of sentence, and also wrote a curious letter to Governor English. He heard his death-sentence with a contemptuous sneer, for he declared he should never be hanged.

On account of his desperate adroitness he was confined in an iron cell; and seeing there no possible chance of escape, he tried to commit suicide by starvation. He refused to take one morsel of food for nine and a half days, and drank water but once in that time! He also tried the second time to starve himself, but after a fast of six days, food was injected into him, which prolonged his miserable life for the gallows. Determined to verify his vow that he never would be hung, he had taken out a piece of wire about three inches long from the rim of his basin, which he rolled in a piece of leather and hid in his body, and to which he attached a string for pulling it out when necessary. In the morning of the fatal Friday on which he was to be hung he took the concealed wire, which he sharpened on the walls of his cell, and *drove it into his heart* so deep that he could not withdraw it, which latter circumstance probably stayed the flow of blood from the heart, and prevented immediate death. In his weak condition he was carried to the gallows, and when in his last moments he was asked if he wished to say anything, replied, "I shall say but few words to-day; a man with three inches of steel in his heart can't say much, nor be expected to!" Thus was this desperate fiend swung from the gallows, with the steel in his obdurate heart of steel—an anomaly in the records of crime!

Gerald Toole was convicted at New Haven, in 1860, of arson, and sentenced to the State prison for life, and in 1862, while in prison, he murdered the warden, Daniel Webster. For this he was sentenced to be hung, and a short time before his execution he wrote a history of his life, and the reasons which impelled him to commit the murder. His mother died in Ireland when he was a child, and in 1858, at the age of twenty, he emigrated to America, where for two years he roamed about New Haven, often being thrown into bad company, and contracting bad habits. He at length hired a small liquor-store, which was soon after set on fire and partly burned; a reward of $200 was offered for the discovery and conviction of the offender. Young Toole asserted that the hope of getting the reward induced others to swear falsely against him, to secure his conviction. On his trial he pleaded not guilty, and his counsel made an able defence, but it was of no avail, and he was sentenced, whether justly or unjustly, for life. At the prison he was placed in the shoe-shop, and for not performing his full allotted daily task (which he asserted was more than he was able to perform), he was severely flogged, and the same task required of him next day. Perceiving no hope of a cessation in his daily miseries, and goaded to desperation, he contrived to secrete a pointed shoe-knife about his person, with which to kill the officer should another attempt be made to flog him. On the day of the murder he either wilfully refused or was physically unable to do the amount required of him; and the warden entering the shop near the close of the day and seeing his task not completed, ordered him to be again whipped. Toole then suddenly sprang upon Captain Webster, and plunged the knife into his chest and abdomen, inflicting wounds from which he died the next day. Toole was tried in May, 1862, and sentenced to be hanged on the 19th of September following, on which day the execution took place in Hartford jail. He was but 24 years of age.

The pamphlet which he wrote was extensively read, and enlisted much public sympathy in his favor. It also caused investigation to be made into the alleged cruelties of the prison, and produced, to some extent, a relaxation of the rigorous discipline which had been previously enforced.

The following statistics have been furnished for this work by the present efficient warden, E. B. Hewes Esq.:—

262 is the present number of convicts, March 25th, 1876. There are 12 more in the county jails under sentence, and soon to be placed in the prison, making the whole number 264.

White males,	221	Under 20 years of age,	29
" females,	3	From 20 to 30 " "	147
Colored males,	27	" 30 " 40 " "	42
" females,	1	" 40 " 50 " "	20
		Over 50 " "	14

CRIMES.

Assault with intent to kill,	12
Murder,	2
" in 2nd degree,	18
Manslaughter,	5
Attempt at rape,	7
Assault with intent at rape,	4
Rape,	5
Assaulting a superior officer,	3
Burglary,	55
Burglary and theft,	5
Breaking and entering,	17
Burning a barn,	4
Bigamy,	4
Drunkeness, disobedience of orders &c.,	7
Desertion,	12

Horse stealing,	13
Arson,	3
Placing obstructions on R. R. track,	4
Robbery,	17
Theft,	30
" from the person,	12
Robbing mail,	1
Breaking jail,	1
Mailing obscene matter,	1
Passing counterfeit money,	1

There are in confinement for life twenty-nine prisoners, which is said to be a larger number proportionally than in any other penitentiary in the United States. Included in the above list are twenty-seven United States' convicts, for which the general government pays this state $2.50 per week for the maintenance of each.

DAILY ROUTINE OF DUTY PERFORMED AT THE CONNECTICUT STATE PRISON BY THE OFFICERS.

At daylight the bell is rung for the officers, who immediately repair to the guard-room. When it is sufficiently light, the deputy-warden gives the signal for manning the walls, and the overseers take their keys, go to their several divisions, and again wait the signal, when they unlock, and march their men, with the lock-step, to their respective shops. The convicts immediately commence work, and also begin at a given point in the shop to wash, which each man does in regular order before the breakfast hour.

At 7 o'clock the bell is rung for breakfast, the convicts stop work, form into a line in their shops, and wait the signal of the bell, when they are marched into the prison yard, and form a line in front of their buckets. At the word *right*, each man turns to the right; the word *up* is given, and each man takes his bucket upon his left arm, when they form into sections in close order, as marched from the shops; and at the word *forward*, they march in the same manner to the hall, where they are seated to hear the reading of the Bible and attend prayers. Thence they are marched round the cells, take their kids containing their breakfast as they pass the kitchen, and are immediately locked up. Each officer then reports the number of men in his charge to the deputy-warden, who, finding it right, gives the signal of "All's well!" the watchmen leave the wall and repair to the guard-room; all the officers then go to their meal, except one in the hall, and one in the guard-room, who are relieved in turn.

From half to three-quarters of an hour is allowed, when they are again, as above, marched to their work, and there remain until twelve o'clock; the signal is again given, they are again marched upon a line, and in the same manner marched into and round the hall, the same as at breakfast, with the exception of service. Time allowed for dinner, one hour in summer, and forty-five minutes in winter. At one o'clock they are again marched to their shops, and work till six P. M., when they again form a line in front of their buckets; the word is given, "One pace in the rear, march," each convict steps one pace back; the officer having charge of each division begins searching, by passing his hands over the arms, body, and legs of the prisoner, and as each man is searched he steps to the front. When all are again in a line, the word is given to *uncover*, and each convict takes the cover from his night bucket; the officers pass and examine them; the words, *cover — right — up — forward*! and they march to the hall, attend prayers, and go to their cells, as in the morning. The officer then in the hall lights up, examines each lock and door, recounts the convicts, and reports the number to the warden or deputy-warden. At half past seven the signal is given, and each convict retires to his cell; the officer again examines the doors, sees that all are abed, and is then relieved by the overseer, taking the first tour, which continues from eight to twelve o'clock. He is then relieved by a watchman, who takes what is called the middle tour, from twelve to four; the watchman taking the morning tour, then relieves him. The above officers are required, while doing duty, to be constantly on their feet, marching round the cells and upon the galleries to see that all is quiet and in good order. If any sickness or disorder takes place, he calls the watchmen, who acquaints the warden or deputy-warden, who immediately repairs to the hall, and takes the necessary measures for relief of the sick or the suppression of disorder.

Duties of the Subordinate Officers.

The Deputy-warden takes the principal charge of the internal affairs, under the direction of the warden; spends the whole day in visiting the several shops and departments; sees that every officer performs his duty; attends to the wants and complaints of the convicts; and has a constant supervision of all the internal operations.

The Clerk assists the warden in keeping the books and other writing: attends generally to the transportation of convicts from the county jails; and when not thus engaged, performs such other duties as are required of him by the warden.

The Overseers, after performing the duty of marching the convicts, as above described, to their shops, remain constantly in them, with their men. They are not allowed to sit down, but must not only remain on their feet, but also exercise the utmost vigilance in seeing that their men work diligently, in order, and silence. In case of sickness or disobedience, they are required to send immediately for the warden or his deputy; they also report in writing, before nine o'clock A. M., all who express a wish to see the physician.

The Watchmen are employed, *all the time*, in duty upon the walls, in the guard-room hall, and hospital, and in waiting upon spectators who visit the prison; they are not allowed to sit, read, or write, while upon any post of duty.

The Gate-keeper has the care of the gate leading into the yard, and takes charge of the out-door hands and work.

The convicts have at all times free and unrestrained access to the warden, and can, whenever they desire to do so, see and converse with the director, or directors, when they visit the prison, but not in the presence of other convicts. All punishments are inflicted by the warden or his deputy. No subordinate officer is allowed to leave the prison day or night, without permission of the warden, or in his absence, the deputy-warden.

DAILY RATIONS.

For breakfast, six days in the week, hash.
" dinner on Monday, corned beef and potatoes.
"   "   " Tuesday, pork and beans.
"   "   " Wednesday, soup.
"   "   " Thursday, corned beef and potatoes.
"   "   " Friday, fish.
"   "   " Saturday, fresh meat stew.
" supper, mush and milk, or mush and molasses.
Coffee each morning, and sufficient bread to each ration.

HISTORICAL SKETCHES OF EAST GRANBY.

This town includes within its limits the old Copper Hill caverns, and contains many of the relics of the copper-mining operations. Here were enacted all the tragical scenes of Tory imprisonment during the Revolution; and for fifty-four years afterward this town furnished the sole prison for Connecticut State convicts. It was set off chiefly from Granby, and in part from Suffield and Windsor Locks, in 1858; Granby having been set off from Simsbury in 1786, and Simsbury from Windsor, in 1670. Thus it appears, these towns were incorporated at periods respectively about a century apart.

The early history of East Granby is involved in that of the bordering towns, so that a general sketch of them all might seem proper; but the prescribed limits of this work do not admit of very extended mention of each, however desirable it might be. Being one of the youngest towns in the State, its official archives do not afford material for voluminous history.

The ancient Indian name of that portion of East Granby, Granby, and Simsbury lying on or near Farmington river, and embracing Copper Hill, was Massaco (Mas-sah′-co). It certainly would have been no disparagement to those towns had the ancient name been continued; and the Tunxis river* which runs through that section would have flowed just as sweetly and sounded as euphoniously as by its later christening, *Farmington*. It is gratifying to know that in later years, with better sense, the old and honored Indian names have been retained in the settlement of many of our western towns, states, and territories.

The fertile valleys in Massaco, the abundance of fish— especially salmon—the great quantity of game, and the upland productions of pitch, tar, and turpentine, attracted at a very early period the people of Windsor; and they were the first colonists who settled in Massaco.

In 1642—about six years after the first settlement of Windsor—the first sale of Massaco land is recorded as follows:

It is ordered that the Governor and Mr. Haynes shall have liberty to dispose of the land upon that part of the Tunxis river called *Massaco*, to such individuals of Windsor as they shall see cause."

In the early disposition of large tracts of land by the infant colony the price was merely nominal, and often a free grant in consideration of the advantage of outpost settlements as a protection against Indian intrusions.

The first Indian deed of land in Massaco was given by the Indian chief Manahanoose to John Griffin, in 1648; and the consideration was that the Indians had destroyed a quantity of pitch and tar owned by Griffin. But, as in other Indian bargains, the title seemed to have been as uncertain as the boundary was indefinite; for soon after, it appears that Mr. Griffin obtained another conveyance of the same territory from three other chiefs who also claimed ownership. From various circumstances it would seem that the area thus purchased comprised a large part of what is now East Granby, Simsbury, and Granby, extending northward to " Southwick Ponds," and the term " more or less " was very liberally construed. This grant from the Indians of so large an extent of country seemed to trouble the other Indian sachems,

---

* Indian signification—Little Crane River.

which induced Griffin some years later to endorse over his title to a committee of the plantation at Windsor—which town claimed a general right to the whole territory. This committee was authorized "to lay out all those lands that are yet undivided at Massaco to such inhabitants of Windsor as desire and need it." The General Court of the colony granted two hundred acres of this to Griffin again, in consideration " that he was the first that perfected the art of making pitch and tar in those parts."

This, with other large grants, comprised many hundred acres owned by Griffin in the region of the Tunxis, making, it is said, a tract three miles square, which is known, even at this day, as " Griffin's Lordship." It lies within the present limits of East Granby, Salmon Brook, and Tariffville. Mr. Griffin was a man of considerable note, was a sergeant in the " train-band," so termed then, and held some civil offices. He carried on the pitch and tar business in the pine-forests for many years—sometimes in company with others—finding a ready sale for his products to the British, for use in their navy. This branch of business in the colonies was encouraged by the mother country, while nearly every other kind of manufacture was encumbered with taxation, so as to prevent competition with her artisans at home.

Whether by accident or design, the savages set fire to Mr. Griffin's pitch and tar. To intimidate them from further depredations, it is said he called them together one day and positively assured them that if they gave him any further trouble he would burn up the Tunxis river and destroy all their fishing! To prove his miraculous power he dipped a bottle of spirit into the river, pretending to fill it with water. Then, with certain incantations, pouring its contents on to a log, he set fire to it—which wonderful deed inspired the savages with such a fear of his omnipotent vengeance, that they manifested a due respect for him ever afterwards.

The Indians in East Granby and other parts of Massaco and Windsor were generally friendly to the white settlers— their confidence having been gained by kindness and usually fair treatment in all business transactions. Their prevailing passion for hunting was very useful to the colonists, who employed them to hunt wolves with which the country was then sadly infested. In January, 1669, it was—

"Voted, to allow the Indians for every wolf they kill and bring their heads in, wampum at 6 a penny 10 shillings; and they that pay it to them must take up in our pay among ourselves with 5 shillings."

So that it appears the wampum of the red-man was considered as rather below par—perhaps bearing a relation to our present paper wampum, when estimated by the standard of gold and silver.

The Indians were conscious that their most dangerous enemies were the powerful, warlike tribes living in Rhode Island and Massachusetts, and they felt that their security in part depended upon making common cause with the settlers against them. The latter made a treaty with the friendly Indians in 1673, stipulating to pay them two yards of cloth for the head of an enemy killed by them, and four yards if delivered alive.

In the spring following several towns in Massachusetts were pillaged and destroyed by the Indians, and many of the people were massacred. This alarmed the settlers of Massaco, for they knew not in what hour the dreaded war-whoop might sound in their ears. The people were ordered to work in companies, armed, and to carry arms to service on Sundays. Two or three houses (or forts) had been built at East Granby, the walls of which were filled with brick to resist attacks from the savages. To these the people fled for safety at every alarm.

The danger finally became so imminent that all the settlers in Simsbury fled to Windsor for safety; and the savages came down from Massachusetts on the 26th of March, 1676, (200 years ago) and burned nearly every house in that part of Massaco, with all the furniture, crops, fences—in fact, everything they could not carry off. This roused the spirit of the settlers, and they resolved to subdue or exterminate them. Several companies of volunteers were organized in Windsor, Massaco, and neighboring places, and with some friendly Indians the war was prosecuted with vigor. Ten or twelve expeditions were made by the colony in less than four months. The results of that campaign are well known. Two hundred and thirty Indians were killed or captured; quantities of grain and muskets were taken; King Philip, the chieftain warrior, was pursued to Mount Hope in Rhode Island and killed; his only son was sold as a slave to the Bermudas; and his once powerful tribe was swept from the face of the earth.

But other hostile tribes still remained in this region; and for nearly half a century afterwards the inhabitants were in constant dread of attacks from the red-skins. As late as 1724, houses and fortifications were maintained in a state of defense at Simsbury, Salmon Brook, and East Granby. At the latter place a garrison of nine men was kept on duty, and a line of scouts was kept up between there and Litchfield to guard against surprises from the Massachusetts tribes.

The following illustrates some of the peculiar methods adopted to hunt down the Indians, by which it appears that the canine race were in better favor than the breeds of generally worthless curs of these days:

"*It is ordered and enacted by this Assembly :—*

"That there shall be allowed and paid out of the publick treasury of this Colony, the sum of fifty pounds in pay, for the bringing up and maintaining of Dogs in the northern frontier towns in this Colony, to hunt after the Indian enemy, and to be improved and ordered for that end by the Committee of War in the county of Hartford, according to their discretion, as soon as may be, who are to procure as many dogs as that money will allow, to be always ready for the Colony's service against the common enemy."

The following interesting narrative was written by the late Noah A. Phelps some years ago. It illustrates the state of constant apprehension endured by our ancestors while the crafty, vindictive lords of the forest were prowling about the country.

CAPTIVITY OF DANIEL HAYES BY THE INDIANS.

In the fall of 1707, Daniel Hayes, at the age of twenty-two years, was taken by the Indians and carried captive into Canada. He resided at Salmon Brook, now the central part of Granby, which, being at that time the northern point of settlement in the town, was peculiarly exposed to sudden invasions by the Indians. The circumstances attending this transaction, as preserved by tradition, are as follows.*

Some two or three years before Hayes was taken, he was at a house-raising in Weatauge, when, very inconsiderately, and out of mere wanton sport, he cut off the tail of a dog belonging to an Indian, who, a stranger and entirely unknown, happened to be present. The master of the dog, though he uttered no complaint, manifested such emotions of ill will and revenge, that Hayes, before they separated, deemed it prudent for himself to attempt to pacify him. He sought therefore a reconciliation, by proposing to drink together, and offered, moreover, reparation for the injury. But the Indian rejected all overtures, and left the ground, evidently in a surly and unreconciled mood of mind, and, probably, with malice and revenge deeply impressed upon his heart. Nothing afterwards being heard of the Indian or his dog, and the circumstance if not forgotten, became unheeded. But the events which follow were supposed to result from this affair.†

On the evening before his capture, there was a corn-husking party at the house of Mr. Hayes, when in the course of conversation, he remarked that early in the ensuing morning, he should endeavor to find his horse, which was feeding in the forests, and, as supposed, westerly of the settlement.

---

*The materials from which this account is compiled, were obligingly communicated to the author by Samuel H. Woodruff and Arden B. Holcomb Esq'rs, of Granby. Of the general correctness of the narrative, no reasonable doubt can be entertained,—as the facts have been derived, not only from the descendants of Mr. Hayes, but also from several aged people, all of whom concur in their statements regarding the main and important features of the transaction.

†Thus goes the story. But the author must be allowed to say for himself, that he very much doubts whether this affair had anything to do with the capture of Hayes, which took place some years afterwards. The Indians, it is well-known, were incited to such deeds by the French in Canada, to whom they carried their captives, and by whom, as is supposed, they were rewarded for the service. The more correct supposition probably is, that the captors came into this weak settlement, to seize and carry off any person who might be thrown in their way, and that they would have taken as readily any other person as Hayes, if an opportunity equally as favorable had occurred.

This conversation, as appears from the sequel, was overheard by Indians who were at that time lurking about the house, and who it is supposed from the information thus obtained, devised their plans of operation for the next morning.

After the family had retired and were asleep, they were awakened by the barking of their dog, which manifested so much uneasiness as to induce Mr. Hayes to leave his bed, and with his dog, to seek for the cause. Supposing the disturbance to have proceeded from the incursion of cattle into the corn-field contiguous to his house, (an ordinary occurrence in those days,) and finding it unmolested, he again sought repose in sleep. But the dog continued restive, and plainly made known by his conduct, that there was something wrong in the neighborhood of the house.

The next morning at an early hour, Mr. Hayes, taking with him a bridle, proceeded into the forests to find his horse. His route led him to pass Stoney Hill, a ridge of land stretching north and south about eighty rods westerly of Salmon Brook street. Upon turning round the south point of this hill, he was seized by three Indians, who sprang upon him from an ambush where they had secreted themselves from view. So suddenly and unexpectedly came this attack upon Hayes, that he was deprived of all power to make resistance, or even any attempt to escape. One Indian seized him by the throat—another enjoined silence by putting a hand over his mouth—whilst the other with a tomahawk raised over his head, enforced obedience and submission. They immediately bound his hands at his back, with the throat-latch of the bridle, and with their captive hastily left the place, taking their course in a northern direction.

Another account states that Hayes was acccompanied by a Mr. Lamson, who being an agile and atheletic man, outran the Indians and effected his escape; that the number of Indians belonging to the party, amounted to five or more; and that the transaction was witnessed by a Mrs. Holcomb, wife of Nathaniel Holcomb, who was in the fields that morning milking, but who, from considerations relating to her own safety, was deterred from returning home, or giving an alarm, until the Indians with their captive had left the place.

Very soon, however, the usual alarm was spread, and a force was raised sufficient to make pursuit. Immediate effort was made to relieve the captive, and punish the aggressors; and notice of the calamity having been sent to Windsor, a larger force came to the rescue from that town. The route taken by the Indians was found and traced, and at times the marks of their tracks appeared so fresh, that strong hopes were entertained of overtaking them. But their superior cunning in such exploits, with their fleetness in passing through the wilderness enabled them to avoid their pursuers, and escape with their prisoner.

In the meantime Hayes, knowing that any symptoms of lagging on his part would probably cost him his life, and supposing, moreover, that in no event would his captors, if closely pursued, suffer him to live, exerted himself to keep up with them. And he soon found he could do this without much fatigue, for he was robust, and accustomed to such travelling. On one occasion during this journey, when his companions wished to test his fleetness, he outstripped them so far that they were on the point of shooting him to stop his progress. He might then have escaped, as he afterwards said, "if he had had his thoughts about him."

On the first night after his capture, the party encamped at the foot of Sodom mountain. Hayes was secured during the night, by being placed upon his back with each arm and ankle strongly fastened to a sapling, and with sticks so crossing his body as to be lain upon by an Indian on each side. He passed most of the nights bound in this manner, during his long march to Canada. On the second day the party crossed Connecticut river, by fording and swimming, and spent the ensuing night at the base of Mount Holyoke.

In this manner they proceeded from day to day, up the valley of Connecticut river and through the wilderness, on their route to Canada. Many incidents occurred which Hayes used to relate. One evening, the little savages belonging to a village where the party had stopped, annoyed him by tickling his feet as he lay before a fire with his arms pinioned as usual. Bearing this annoyance as long as his patience would allow, he attempted to get rid of his tormentors by using his feet in self-defense—during which process some of them were kicked into the fire. He expected nothing short of death for this aggression, but was agreeably surprised when the fathers of the burnt children, instead of offering violence, patted him on his shoulders and exclaimed "boon!"*

They were nearly thirty days on this journey, during all which time the sufferings of poor Hayes were excessive, and almost without intermission. Subjected to hard toil through each day, with no sustenance save what the forests and rivers furnished, and deprived at night of rest by the manner of binding his limbs, he had that to sustain which in most cases would have brought the sufferer to the grave. But Hayes if he must be a victim, determined that he at least would not voluntarily contribute to hasten the sacrifice. He possessed that happy faculty of making at all times, the best of his condition. His cheerfulness, though assumed— his ability to endure fatigue and hardships—and his apparent stoical indifference to his fate, secured the good opinion of his comrades, and tended to lighten his burdens, and possibly, to prolong his life. Indulgence in despondency could bring no relief, and would as he well knew, but render more bitter the cup of his afflictions. He very wisely therefore made up his mind "to make a virtue of necessity," by submitting with the best possible grace to that fate which he too well knew awaited him.

The Indians told him, on the journey, of their lying about

---

*If this word is correctly handed down, it was intended probably, for the French word *bon*, and used on this occasion to express approbation. The northern Indians, at this time were in the habit of using a few words derived from the French.

his house on the night before he was taken, and of overhearing the conversation relating to his intention to proceed, on the next morning, into the wilderness to find his horse; which information, thus obtained, induced them to lie in wait at Stoney Hill in order to capture him.

When they arrived at the great Indian encampment on the borders of Canada, the prisoner was delivered over to the council of the nation, to be disposed of as they should adjudge. By their decision, he was doomed to undergo the painful ordeal of "*running the gauntlet.*" Being stripped to his skin, and annointed according to custom, he commenced the course; and after many flagellations and hard knocks received, when approaching near the end of the line, being exhausted and faint, he bolted from the course to avoid a blow from an upraised war-club, and sought safety by fleeing into a wigwam, at the door of which sat a superannuated and infirm squaw. He was pursued, but the squaw proclaimed the house *sacred*, and its inmates protected from injury. By her intercession, and especially by the deference paid to a place thus sanctified according to the rites of Indian superstition, "the appetite of the savage for blood was stayed."

The squaw, whose husband and only son had fallen in war, claimed the captive, and adopted him as her son. She was destitute, and so infirm as to be unable to walk. Haynes, in addition to minor duties, was compelled to provide for her sustenance and fuel. He administered to her wants, and devoted to her the kindest attentions,—and she, in return, evinced her gratitude, by calling him *her son!* He lived in this family about five years: and although, during this time, he fared better, perhaps, than most Indian captives, yet existence, in his then condition, had for him but few charms. and the future unveiled to his view no cheering prospect. He was in bondage, compelled to adopt the customs and modes of life of savages, and was deprived of almost every comfort deemed necessary by civilized people. Besides, he could entertain no reasonable hope of being restored to his home and kindred—and more than all, his life was at the mercy, whim, or caprice, of savage masters.

One of the tasks imposed upon him in the winter season, was to draw upon a sled his Indian mother to such places as she wished to visit, and especially to the feasts and council assemblages of her tribe. Upon occasion of a "dog feast," which by the usages of her people, all were expected to attend, he proceeded with her, in this manner, until, ascending a hill which was steep and slippery, he found his strength, when put to its utmost power, barely adequate to make any headway. By perseverance and exertion, however, he was enabled to reach nearly the summit of the hill, when he slipped and fell; and either by design, or inability to hold on, left the sled, with its mortal load, to find the bottom of the declivity without a pilot—secretly wishing, no doubt, that her appetite for riding would be cured by this trip. In this perilous adventure, the sled struck a stump near the foot of the hill, which capsized the squaw, who was severely injured by the fall. Whether an accident or not, Hayes professed much sorrow for the disaster, and managed the affair so adroitly, that he escaped every imputation of blame, and continued to retain the confidence and good opinion of the Indians.

Shortly after this event, he was sold to a Frenchman in Montreal, through the agency, it is said, of a Papist priest. His new master was very kind, and allowed him many of the necessaries, with some of the luxuries, of life, of which he had been so long deprived. Learning that Hayes was by trade a weaver, he started him in this business, and by allowing him a share of the profits, Hayes was enabled, in the course of about two years, to earn money enough to purchase his freedom. The good Frenchman not only emancipated him, but supplied him with clothes, provisions, and a half-breed guide to conduct him safely through the warring tribes on his journey homeward. The guide proceeding with him as far as Mount Holyoke, pointed out to him the smoke of his friends, "the pale faces," wished him a happy return to his family, and departed in another direction to wend his way back to Canada. In about twenty-five days after leaving Montreal, Hayes had the happiness to reach his home, and to exchange hearty greetings and congratulations with his friends, to whom he appeared almost "as one raised from the dead."

Thus, after an absence of about seven years, the captive was restored to freedom, a home, and a happy circle of relatives and friends. He had heard nothing from his family since his capture, nor had they received any tidings of him, though they either knew, or had good reason to suppose, that he had been taken and carried off by the Indians. His friends had flattered themselves, for a long while, that he would be spared to return to them, but his long absence had extinguished every vestige of hope, and he had for some time been given up as lost.

With buoyant spirits, renovated courage, and unshaken resolution, he set himself to the task of making up for the *lost time* he had spent with the Indians. His constitution, naturally robust, had suffered nothing by his long captivity, and his ambition had lost none of its fire. He married, settled down upon a farm, and within a short time, became a thriving agriculturist. In 1720, he built a house on the east side of Salmon Brook Street, in the lower or southern part of the street, which was standing until within a few years past. In this house religious meetings were held during some four or five years before the erection of the first meeting-house of that society, in 1743.

Mr. Hayes became a prominent citizen, was often employed in civil affairs, and during many years, was a pillar in the church at Salmon Brook, of which he was a member at its organization. He lived to see the infant settlement, so long exposed to Indian barbarities, a populous village, with no crafty enemy to disturb its repose, and strong enough, had danger existed, to protect its inhabitants from plunder or capture. But, long before his death, all Indian difficulties had ceased.

He died, 1756, at the age of seventy-one, and was buried in the cemetery at the north end of the village. A red freestone monument marks the spot of his last resting-place, on which is inscribed the following epitaph:

> HERE LIES YE BODY OF
> MR. DANIEL HAYES,
> Who served his Generation in steady course of Probity and Piety,
> and was a lover of Peace, and God's Public Worship;
> And being satisfied with Long life,
> left this world with a Comfortable Hope of life Eternal,
> Sept. 3d, 1756,
> in ye 71 year of his Age.

In Oct. 1713 the General Assembly of the Colony voted as follows:

"Upon consideration of the petition of Daniel Hayes of Symsbury, having been taken by the Indian enemy and carried captive to Canada—praying for some relief: This Assembly do grant unto the petitioner the sum of seven pounds, to be paid him out of the public treasury of this Colony."

The Red-Men who, for unknown generations, roved among the forests and occupied the fine fisheries of Massaco are now departed forever. "Slowly and sadly they climb the distant mountains and read their doom in the setting sun," while the Pale-Faces follow in their wake, and transform their hunting-grounds into peaceful and pleasant abodes of a happier civilization.

> "'Tis not two centuries since they—
> The red-men—traversed here;
> And o'er these pleasant hills and vales
> Pursued the bounding deer.
> Yet of their moral weal or woe
> No trace is left to-day,
> For, like the foam upon the wave,
> They all have passed away!"

Some fifty or sixty years ago a straggling Indian and squaw were occasionally to be met with in this vicinity, depending mainly upon selling a few baskets and mats, or upon the charity of the inhabitants, for support. In the vicinity of Copper Hill and other parts of East Granby, and in neighboring towns there are often dug up Indian relics, such as arrow-heads, stone axes, stone pots, mortars and pestles for pounding corn, and rude weapons of war.

REVOLUTIONARY INCIDENTS.

East Granby's limits furnished—in proportion to her then

sparse settlement—a full quota of patriotic soldiers for the War of the Revolution, and also for the war of 1812. Some thirty soldiers volunteered or were drafted in the Revolution, and a number of them served during the entire war. Colonel Andrew Hillyer, a native of East Granby, and father of General Charles T. Hillyer, of Hartford, was a sergeant in the Indian war and was at the siege of Havana, thirteen years before the Revolution. He then enlisted in that war—was a lieutenant, afterwards captain of dragoons, and served eight years. After the war he was colonel of the militia. He died at East Granby in 1828, aged 86.

One of the notables of East Granby was the Honorable Samuel Woodruff. At the age of 17, while at Yale College, hearing of the efforts of the Americans to capture Burgoyne's army at Saratoga, he with several other students hastened with all possible speed to the scene of conflict, arriving there in time to participate in that decisive battle, and to witness the ceremonies of the surrender. He was for some years a judge of the court of Hartford county, and one of the overseers of Newgate prison. In 1828 he was appointed a commissioner to distribute supplies to the suffering Greeks after their war with the Turks, and at the age of 70 crossed the Atlantic and accomplished that misson of charity. His remarkably retentive memory, stored with a fund of historic facts, together with his ready application of anecdote and sallies of wit and humor, made his society instructive and agreeable to all classes. He died at East Granby, in 1850, aged nearly 91.

Lemuel Bates was a captain during the Revolution, and participated in several battles. For many years Captain Bates kept a tavern in the north part of East Granby, in the house where his grandson, Wm. H. Bates, now lives. The merry old gentleman was fond of fighting his battles over again by relating his reminiscences of those interesting times. After the surrender of Burgoyne, with his once splendid army of 10,000 men, at Saratoga, several detachments of the British prisoners of war were marched through East Granby, and a portion of them bivouacked on the premises of Captain Bates. "The British had plenty of money," said Captain Bates, "to pay for the best we had; and my folks were kept busy in distributing pitchers and pails of cider among them. At night all the floors in my tavern were spread over with them."

Another portion of the British captives encamped on the premises of Captain Roswell Phelps,* near the centre of East Granby. These prisoners of war were an interesting sight, and excited an inspiring curiosity in all this region.

At one time several teams laden with specie, *en route* from Boston to Philadelphia, halted for the night at Captain Bates's. The specie had been borrowed from France; which nation was then fraternally aiding us in our struggle. It was enclosed in strong plank boxes, drawn by thirteen teams, well guarded; and amounted to several millions of dollars.

Among those captives in Burgoyne's army was one by the name of Charles Stevens. He belonged to one of the companies of grenadiers who were selected as being the tallest and most martial in appearance of the British troops. He was about 6½ feet in height, according to the author's recollection of him. In that connection he used to remark, "I was among the *short* men in my company, and so was placed on the left of the line."

It came to pass that Stevens took to himself a wife and settled in East Granby. Being under the necessity of "turning his sword into a ploughshare and his spear into a pruning hook," he served as a day laborer for farmers in the neighborhood. He was particularly expert in digging ditches, and usually went by the name of "the ditcher." Two maidens of the neighborhood meeting him one day innocently saluted him with—" Good morning, Mr. Ditcher."

The old veteran turned upon the damsels with flashing

---

* Captain Phelps went into the service at the age of 16. His son, Roswell H., now lives upon a part of the same farm, at the age of '88, in robust health, and brings down the scales at 261: and *his* son (the author of this work) is the sixth generation that has resided on a part of said premises.

eye and informed them that he did not acknowledge that title, exclaiming with a haughty look "I am a grenadier of General Burgoyne's army and was a big man before you were born!"

One of East Granby's sons who rose to distinction was the Hon. Walter Forward.* When at the age of 20, his father removed with his family (in 1803) to Ohio; and, young Forward, on foot, drove an ox-team laden with household goods, as was the custom of travelling then. He afterwards removed to Pennsylvania, where he engaged in the practice of law, became a Member of Congress, Secretary of the United States' Treasury, and Minister to Denmark. At the time of his death he was Chief Judge of the court in Pennsylvania. He died at the age of 69.

The following is a list of those from East Granby who were engaged in the Revolution, and in the War of 1812—though there may have been others whose names are not herein enumerated:

REVOLUTIONARY SOLDIERS.

Col. Andrew Hillyer, Hon. Samuel Woodruff, Capt. Isaac Owen, Capt. Lemuel Bates, Capt. Matthew Griswold, Capt. Roswell Phelps, Sergt. Richard Gay, Joel Clark, Reuben Clark, Zopher Bates, John Forward, Hezekiah Holcomb, John Cornish, Asahel Holcomb, Thomas Stevens, Jesse Clark, Joseph Clark, John Thrall, Luke Thrall, David Eno, Reuben Phelps, Samuel Clark, Joseph Dyer.

WAR OF 1812.

Dan Forward, Joseph Cornish, Appollos Gay, Orson P. Phelps, Calvin Holcomb, Alex. Hoskins, Wm. K. Thrall, Eratus Holcomb, Gurdon Gould, Peultha Clark, Uriah Holcomb, Elihu Andruss, John G. Munn, Alex. Clark, Abiel Clark, Chandler Owen, Sardius Thrall, Charles Buck, Elihu Phelps, Ephraim Shaylor, William Rockwell, Jesse Clark, Jr.

---

* A sister of his, Mrs. Hannah Clark, now resides in East Granby, at the venerable age of 91—being the oldest person in town—and in fair enjoyment of her naturally strong mental faculties

Society Matters.

The "Society of Turkey Hills," in East Granby, was formed in 1736, and comprised, at the time, forty-six families. The first church was built in 1738, the site having been previously fixed by a committee appointed by the General Assembly. There had been for several years previously such a bitter controversy over the formation of societies and location of sites for churches in Granby, and the societies had become so much disorganized that the Assembly refused to appoint any Justices of the Peace in the town for three years—1731 to 1734. The old church remained in a rough condition for about half a century when, in 1794, it was thoroughly repaired and a steeple built. In 1830 having stood for ninety-two years, it was taken down, and a handsome one, built of stone, was erected on a new site, in 1831.

For several years previous to the removal of the prison from Newgate, the State united with the society of Turkey Hills in employing a chaplain to preach a part of each Sunday in the prison chapel, where all who desired were allowed to assemble in the same room with the convicts.

It is interesting to look over the ecclesiastical records of East Granby just one hundred years ago, and note the prevailing habits and customs of those Revolutionary times. In 1776 it appears that Rev. Aaron Booge was settled* as a minister in that society, and the following is on the society records.

"Oct. 22d 1776—*Voted* to give Mr. Aaron Booge Two hundred Pounds as a settlement, to be paid in four Equal payments, to be paid in four yes after settlement.—Also voted to give Mr. Booge as a Sallery, Fifty Pounds a year for ye first four yes, and then to rise to Sixty pounds, and it is to be understood that ye people of s^d Society shall have Liberty yearly, to Pay the one half of s^d Sellery in Wheat, Rye, & Indian Corn, or either of them, at ye common market Price.— Voted also to give ye s^d Mr. Booge, Twenty Seven Cords of good Siseable Wood a year, yearly ; and it is to be understood that Less answering the end, then the whole is not to be Required, and it is to be understood That the above Payments are to be equivalent to the Present Lawful money of the State of Conecticut ; Silver being Six Shillings and eight Pence to the ounce, or to be p^d in bills of

---

*As a fit preparation for the day of ordination the society voted to appoint *seventeen tavernkeepers!*

Public credit, & grain as above mentioned equivalent thereto."—Two years later the price of Wheat was voted by the society "at 5ˢ, Rye at 3ˢ, and Corn at 2·6 a bushel."

This Rev. gentleman afterwards distinguished himself in the War of 1812, as Chaplain in the army under Gen. Jackson. He was an enthusiastic admirer of the old hero, and was fond of relating his adventures while in the army.

The way to reach Copper Hill.

As the old caverns and vicinity will continue to be a place of classic interest, the tourist and visitor will ask how to reach there. The N. Y., N. H. & Hartford R. R., Shelburne Falls Branch, passes about one mile west, and the nearest station on that road being at Granby, two and one-fourth miles southwest. The Central New England R. R. passes through Tariffville about three miles south, and also East Granby, one and one-fourth miles distant, this being the nearest railroad station of any. Windsor Locks, seven miles east, is on the N. Y., N. H. & Hartford R. R. From either of these places, teams can be had to convey travellers to the mines.

There can be seen most of the old prison buildings,—the guardhouse, treadmill, and several of the workshops &c., all bearing marks of decay and dilapidation. The old stonewall enclosure surmounted with watch-towers is standing, and the moat or ditch, once fourteen feet deep, still yawns above the subterraneous excavations. Were this weird place with all its eventful associations located in Europe, it would be a special and marked object for description in the writings of tourists; and the wonder is that people, even in this State know so little of the classic features of Newgate. Says Nordhoff, "There have been Americans who saw Rome before they saw Niagara." Upon the craggy rocks which overhang it on the east, there is a bold, magnificent view, of great scope to the north, south, and west, and if a few foresttrees were cleared away on the eastern slope of the ledge, a splendid panoramic view of great extent and beauty would be unfolded, the whole equalling, if not surpassing, the celebrated Wadsworth tower. The ascent to the cliff, a little south of it, is not difficult, and with little labor a more convenient flight of steps could be made out of the quanties of stones and rock, lying loosely along its sides and base.

The caverns, only about one hundred rods distant from the ledge, will remain for ages to come, and continue to grow in interest during the flight of years. Some of the buildings now falling to decay, could be repaired and preserved, and the old guard-house made a place for entertainment. If put in proper condition, the place would attract a large number to explore the mines, to view the romantic scenery in the vicinity and surrounding country, and enjoy the invigorating benefits of the pure mountain air. The piscatorian could indulge his sportive pastime at Southwick ponds, lying about four miles to the north, and comprising hundreds of acres in extent, where a small steamboat is employed during the summer, for the use of the numerous pleasure parties who meet there for fishing, clambaking, dancing, etc.

www.ingramcontent.com/pod-product-compliance
Lightning Source LLC
Chambersburg PA
CBHW020145170426
43199CB00010B/888